THE NEW ENGLAND MEETING HOUSES

OF THE SEVENTEENTH CENTURY

The

New England Meeting Houses

of the

Seventeenth Century

BY

MARIAN CARD DONNELLY

Wesleyan University Press

MIDDLETOWN, CONNECTICUT

Copyright © 1968 by Wesleyan University

Library of Congress catalog card number: 68–27546

Manufactured in the United States of America

FIRST EDITION

For
C. W. and C. L. V. M.

Contents

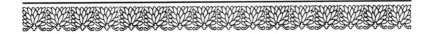

List of Illustrations

THE NEW ENGLAND MEETING HOUSES

OF THE SEVENTEENTH CENTURY

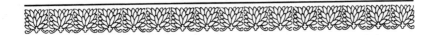

Preface

IN THE steady succession of studies which are published on early American history and culture, frequent mention is made of the New England meeting houses of the seventeenth century. The importance of these buildings in New England is a reflection of the role played by the Congregational Church in public and cultural affairs, and their significance to the communities is indicated in part by the fact that hardly any extant town records fail to include references to their construction or maintenance.

In most cases, such mention does not provide descriptions of specific buildings, nor does it account for their characteristics. Of the more strictly architectural discussions, a few have concentrated on the meeting houses without reference to other relevant building types, and when attempts have been made to relate the meeting houses to contemporary religious architecture elsewhere, this has been done in general terms and without careful chronological and structural comparisons.

The present study has been made in order to provide at least an introduction to a more meticulous scrutiny of the New England meeting houses in relation to their English and Continental contemporaries. This preliminary investigation indicates that the meeting houses were apparently not linked to fashionable developments in the English Renaissance or to experimental Protestant architecture in northern Europe, but were derived naturally from late medieval English village traditions.

Since this study was completed, Professor Richard Krautheimer's discussion of Early Christian basilicas, in his *Early Christian and Byzantine Architecture* (Baltimore: Penguin Books, 1965), has contributed a striking parallel to the history of the meeting houses. The "medley of sacred and secular" which he finds in the basilica (p. 21) appears to have been precisely the mechanism that produced the meeting houses. This parallel is peculiarly appropriate in view of the Puritans' frequently avowed desire to return to primitive Christian practices. Their merging of familiar sacred and secular forms and uses was certainly not consciously inspired by any knowledge of Early Christian architecture. The parallel is not therefore meaningful as a direct explanation of the source of style, but it is illuminating as a corrective to attempts to force the New England meeting houses into an avant-garde context to which they did not belong. And as the Early Christian basilica has been seen as the last new creation of classical architecture, so may the meeting house be seen as one of the final contributions of medieval architecture.

This opinion has been reached after several years' study of the meeting houses. My previous work in Early American architecture under the guidance of Professor Clarence Ward began a lively interest in seventeenth-century problems, which was subsequently furthered by work on the meeting houses themselves under the late Professor Carroll L. V. Meeks, who knew of the completion of this study before his death. I am much indebted to both for their sustained interest and encouragement.

A study of this kind is not possible without the generous assistance of many librarians and archivists. Town clerks and local librarians and historians all over New England have made town records and local histories available. The patient ingenuity of Miss Helen M. Smith, in charge of Interlibrary Loan at the University of Chicago, made it possible to verify many details for which travel to New England was impossible. Mrs. Elizabeth M. Brown of Guilford, Conn., also very kindly helped with verification of dates. The index was prepared with the help of Mrs. Lorraine Purnell.

Permission to use photographs was kindly granted by the Lutherhalle, Wittenberg; the Archives Municipales, Lyon; the Bibliothèque, Geneva; the Kongelige Bibliothek, Copenhagen; the Harvard College Library; The National Monuments Record, London; the Phelps Stokes Collection of the New York Public Library; the Yale University Library; the Massachusetts Historical Society, Boston; the Pilgrim Society, Plymouth; and Mr. Geoffrey N. Wright, Limpley Stoke, Bath, Somerset, England. Permission to reprint illustrations was granted by the editors of *Old Time New England* and the *Journal of the Society of Architectural Historians.* Photographs from the author's negatives were prepared by Mr. John M. Rosenthal, and drawings from the author's conjectural sketches were prepared by Mr. Robert W. Koster.

In order to avoid an indigestible presentation of repetitive detail, the great volume of information on the meeting houses has been analyzed, and the results of this analysis, rather than a complete reporting of the data, are presented in the text. The principal sources of information are given in Appendix A and a list of the buildings, with additional notes, in Appendix B. This material, and the conclusions regarding it, is recorded here in hope of increasing the breadth and accuracy of understanding of the Puritan meeting houses.

M. C. D.

Eugene, Oregon
April 1968

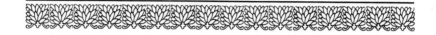

CHAPTER ONE

New England Meeting Houses of the Great Migration, 1630–1642

FOR MORE than eighty years historians of American religious, social, and architectural traditions have described and analyzed the Puritan meeting houses of early New England. Whether intrigued by a possible correlation between Puritan doctrines and modes of construction, by the patterns of early New England life as reflected in Puritan worship, or by the ways in which English medieval building techniques were adapted for religious architecture in the New World, these historians have usually shared one especial enthusiasm: they have been investigating a *Puritan* phenomenon.

Because these meeting houses have virtually all disappeared and the available information on individual buildings is difficult to obtain, there has been a tendency to discuss the Puritan meeting houses in general terms and to devote considerable attention to the builders as well. This has led to a search for the motivation of the builders, at which point the conflicts of mutually exclusive theories begin.

Since opinions concerning these motives have been influenced more by the changing points of view and interests among scholars than by significant increases in knowledge about the meeting houses, some useful contribution may be made by a more intense study of the buildings themselves. If the Puritan meeting houses are investigated in more meticulous detail and their position in

6

the history of American architecture more clearly established, it may be possible to resolve some of the controversies.

Among the views held as to the origins of the New England meeting houses, one of the most popular has been that this type of building was introduced fully understood, though not necessarily fully elaborated, by the colonists immediately upon their arrival in America and that this was done in deliberate, conscious rejection of the parish churches of England. A second view, sometimes presented as a corollary to the first, has been that since a group of English dissenters spent some years of refuge in Holland before settling at Plymouth, Mass., their acquaintance with Dutch Protestant architecture provided the necessary point of departure for the design of meeting houses in New England.

The critical period, then, according to these proposals, would be the years of the Great Migration, about 1630 to 1642, or from the arrival of John Winthrop to the outbreak of the Civil War in England. During this time a basic solution to the problem of constructing a building for public meetings and worship should have been reached. No buildings or drawings of them remain, but substantial quantities of written records attest that the meeting house as a distinct architectural type did indeed make its appearance in these years, and that much can be learned about their structural details. Forty meeting houses were built in these first years from 1630 to 1642: twenty-nine in the Massachusetts Bay Colony, six in Connecticut, and one on Long Island, while four towns replaced their first meeting houses with second buildings.

Although these figures indicate that religious factors were prominent in their minds, the early settlers in New England did not always build meeting houses immediately upon settlement at new town sites, nor can it be shown that they intended from the beginning to build "meeting houses" as distinct from "churches." The documentary evidence is rather to the contrary.

The Puritan migration to Massachusetts Bay was not wholly impulsive, but came after twenty-five years of English fishing and colonizing enterprises in New England, none of which had been permanently successful.[1] The closest forerunner of the Puritan settlements was the fishing venture at Cape Ann, undertaken by a group from Dorchester, England, whose charter (January 1, 1623/24), granted by the Council for New England, included provision for "ffyve hundred acres of free land adioyning to the said Bay to be ymployed for public vses as for the building of a Towne, Scholes, Churches, Hospitalls...."[2] This charter reflected an already strong religious inclination among the members of the Dorchester Company.[3]

Some of the English trading and plantation documents included only provision for public worship or the maintenance of a minister, but not for a place of worship, as in the charter of the Eastland Company (1599). The English merchants of the Eastland Company at Elbing, Germany, worshipped in the residence which they rented.[4] The *Orders and Conditions* of the Ulster plantation (February, 1608/9) did specify: "That there shall be a convenient number of Parishes and Parish Churches with sufficient Incumbents in every county; and that the Parishioners shall pay all their Tithes in kind to the Incumbents of the said Parish Churches."[5] The later *Advices set down by the Commissioners* for Ulster (1610) provided even more exactly:

> 5. To set out a convenient place for a church-yard, in which a church may be built....
> 11. The Deputy and council to take orders for the peopling and inhabiting towns, erecting schools, and building churches, so far as the means of the country will yield.[6]

By contrast, the *Articles of Agreement* for Londonderry (January 28, 1609/10) indicated that churches were expected but did not definitely instruct that they be built: "It is agreed that the City shall have the Patronage of all the Churches as well within the said City of the Derry and Town of Coleraine as in the lands to be undertaken by them."[7]

The second and third charters of the Virginia Company of London (May 23, 1609 and March 12, 1612) provided for land and maintenance of ministers but made no mention of places of worship.[8] Similarly, the treatise of Richard Eburne (1624) spoke of the "one sort of people most needful of all others to be had, I mean, ministers of the Word of God," and suggested how they

8

were to be supported, but said nothing about building churches.[9]

When the Dorchester fishing enterprise was not successful, a joint stock company was organized under the leadership of the Rev. John White of Dorchester. This New England Company was granted "a patent of some lands in the Massachusetts Bay" by the Council for New England (March 19, 1627/28),[10] and some settlers went to Massachusetts with John Endicott as the Governor in New England.

A year later (March 4, 1628/29) a charter was granted to the "Governor and Company of the Massachusetts Bay in New England."[11] There is no mention of possible building programs in this charter, which was written more in terms of a commercial trading company than of a plantation. The fate of this charter was of the greatest importance. By the secret "Cambridge Agreement" of August 26, 1629, those stockholders intending to go to New England bought all the shares in the Company and determined to assume entire control of the venture in New England, taking the Charter with them. The commercial and ultimately political separatism of this move, combined with the religious independence already starting in Massachusetts Bay, prepared the way for the establishment of the theocratic commonwealth of Massachusetts.

John White and the other leaders of the enterprise were Puritans and, unlike the Separatists, preached in the parish churches in England when possible. Shortly after the "Cambridge Agreement," while the stockholders were meeting in London (on October 16 at the home of the former London governor, Matthew Cradock), they discussed "building of fforts" and "building convenyent churches," both to be paid by public funds, one half from joint stock and one half from the planters.[12] On February 10, 1629/30, there was again talk of the costs of "building of churches & ffortyfycačons."[13] And that, as far as it seems possible to determine, is the last time that the settlers of Massachusetts Bay went on record as intending to build "churches."

Previously, on April 17, 1629, Matthew Cradock had written to John Endicott that beaver trade profits should be used for "building houses for God's worship" and forts.[14] The next men-

9

tion of a building designated as a place of worship is in the *Journal* of John Winthrop, where on March 19, 1631/32, he speaks of the "new meeting house" at Dorchester, Mass.[15] From this time on, references in the New England documents are to "meeting houses."

Winthrop's *Journal* appears to contain the earliest surviving use of the term "meeting house." Yet his diary was a private document, and does not necessarily contain the first use of this term. More probably it was by then common enough for Winthrop to have used it automatically in noting the events of the day. Later, on August 5, 1633, he speaks of beginning the "meeting house" at Boston.[16] The term has not been found in English writings until much later. Puritans had been meeting for worship in private houses since the middle of the sixteenth century, but all references to these meetings seem to be to "private places," "private houses," or "Mr. X's house." If the term "meeting house" was used in England by anyone, Puritan or Anglican, before the settlement of Massachusetts Bay, this use has yet to be brought to light, and a New England origin for the expression seems likely according to present knowledge.

According to tradition, a frame house was taken by the Dorchester Company to Cape Ann in 1624 and used by the authorities.[17] Roger Conant, who had been an uncomfortable Puritan in Separatist Plymouth, became manager or local Governor of the settlement at Cape Ann in 1625. A year later, in the autumn of 1626, the settlement was moved to Salem (then called Naumkeag), and Conant's house was moved too. Richard Brackenbury, in 1680, recalled "an house built at Cape Ann, which Walter Knight and the rest said they built for Dorchester men: and so I was sent with them to Cape Ann to pull down the said house for Mr. Endicott's use, the which we did."[18] Brackenbury, writing more than fifty years after the event, evidently forgot that the house was first used by Conant, since Endicott did not land in Salem until September 6, 1628. In the letter from Matthew Cradock to Endicott, quoted above, Cradock also speaks of the ministers to be sent to New England, Francis Bright, Francis Higginson, and Samuel Skelton, and says: "In convenient tyme lett there bee houses built them."[19] With Cradock's separate reference to "houses for God's worship" and to dwellings for the ministry, it can probably be assumed that in Salem the minister's house was not intended to be the place of worship.

Higginson and Skelton arrived in Salem at the end of June 1629, and a church was organized at Salem on August 6, 1629. Higginson later recorded that "when we came first to Nehumkek, we found about half a score houses, and a faire house newly built for the Governor."[20] It was this "faire house" that was used as the meeting house, as James Cudworth wrote to Dr. Stoughton in England in December 1634: "His [Endicott's] house, being the largest, is their meeting-house, where they are as yet but 60 persons."[21] That is, the dwelling originally provided for the Governor, not that for the minister, was used for meetings in Salem, the house of the civil rather than the religious authority.

Previously in London, John Winthrop had been chosen Governor on October 20, 1629. He started from Southampton in March 1630, on the *Arbella,* together with settlers in three additional boats. They landed at Salem on June 12, 1630. This was the beginning of the Great Migration of 20,000 settlers to New England in the 1630s.

Winthrop and his company moved at once to Charlestown, where a congregation was organized with the ministers John Wilson and George Phillips, "their meeting-place being abroad under a tree, where I have heard Mr. Wilson and Mr. Phillips preach many a good sermon."[22] A gesture of conformity was made at the gathering of the Charlestown church on August 27, 1630, according to Cotton Mather:

. . . although he [Mr. Wilson] now submitted unto an ordination with an imposition of such hands as were by the church invited so to pronounce the benediction of Heaven upon him, yet it was done with a protestation by all, that it should be only as a sign of his election to the charge of his new flock, without any intention that he should thereby renounce the ministry he had received in England.[23]

While at Charlestown, Winthrop and the leaders of the congregation lived in the "Great House" which had been built in 1628 by Thomas Graves. The congregation soon divided, Winthrop going to Boston and Sir Richard Saltonstall, who had emigrated with Winthrop, going to Watertown. For the ministers it was ordered on August 23, 1630, "that houses should be built for them with convenient speede, att the publique charge. Sʳ Rich: Saltonstall vndertook to see it done att his plantaçon for Mʳ Phillips, and Mʳ Goûnʳ, att the other plantaçon, for Mʳ Wilson."[24]

The settlers remaining in Charlestown worshipped with those who went to Boston until 1632, when the Charlestown portion formed their own church on November 2. In April 1633, it was agreed

> that the sum of ten pounds be collected of the said inhabitants, and be paid to John Winthrop, Esq. governour, and the rest of the gentlemen interested in the great house built in anno 1628, by Mr. Graves and the company's servants; which is for the purchase of the said house, now the publick meeting house in this town; all which was accordingly done.[25]

In 1635 the meeting house was sold to Robert Long:

> Mr. Long was granted to have the Great House wholly when we shall be provided of another meeting-house, and to pay £30, and for the present to have the south end, and so much of the chamber as the deacons can spare, and when the congregation leave the house, the deacons are to have the plank and the boards which lie over the chamber with all the forms below and benches.[26]

The new meeting house must have been ready by 1638, when there is a reference to the "old meeting house."[27]

The "Great House" at Charlestown was evidently a regular timber dwelling in which the large chamber or parlor was used for meetings. The same arrangement was made by the Boston congregation, which first met at Winthrop's house. On September 7, 1630, "it was ordered that euy third Tuesday there should be a Court of Assistants helde at the Goûñoʳs howse, (for the tyme being) to begin att 8 of the clocke in the morneing."[28] Then

Mr. Wilson left for England in March 1631, and on the eve of his departure "Mr. Coddington and Mr. Wilson, and divers of the congregation, met at the governor's and there Mr. Wilson, praying and exhorting the congregation to love, etc., commended them to the exercise of prophecy in his absence."[29]

Finally, in 1632, "the congregation at Boston and Charlestown began the meeting house at Boston, for which, and Mr. Wilson's house, they had made a voluntary contribution of about one hundred and twenty pounds."[30] Here began the long history of religious architecture in Boston.

At Watertown there was also some delay in building a separate meeting house. The order for building a house for the minister, John Phillips, has been noted. John Masters wrote to Lady Barrington in England on March 14, 1630/31, that "Sir Richard Saltonstall hath also much building at his own house, and fencing, ploughing, and planting, and also to help build the new city, and, first, for a house for God to dwell in."[31] A "rate" for the meeting house at Watertown is first recorded on August 23, 1634, which suggests that it may not have been built until that year or more probably the next (*T.R.*, 1).[32] Possibly at the beginning Mr. Phillips' house and the "house for God to dwell in" were the same.

At Strawbery Banke (now Portsmouth), N.H., money was voted on May 25, 1640, for "a parsonage house with a chapple thereunto united," a combination known in England.[33] As late as 1683 such a building was proposed at Enfield, Conn. (*T.R.*, I, 77) At Scituate, Mass., meetings seem to have started at the time of settlement in 1634 at the house of James Cudworth,[34] and similar arrangements were evidently made in some of the Connecticut towns.[35]

Whether or not any of these houses were called "meeting houses" before 1632, by that year a separate, specific meeting house was clearly in the minds of the settlers. The one at Boston, mentioned by Winthrop, is one of the earliest of which there seems to be any record. Nothing is known about it except that by 1639 it was "decayed and too small," and it was replaced in 1640.[36]

No extensive records have survived for any single one of the meeting houses built during this first period; from the scattered bits of information which are available, it is possible to form some idea of what they were like and of the possible variations among them. The meeting house at Cambridge, Mass., first mentioned on December 24, 1632, was probably square, as the town voted in March 1649/50, to repair it with a "4:square rooffe" (*T.R.*, 85). The first meeting house at Roxbury, Mass., was on the other hand probably rectangular, since instructions for clapboards and galleries in 1656 and 1659 speak of the "ends" of the building (*T.R.*, I, March 19, 1655/56; February 11, 1658/59). Galleries were added to a number of meeting houses sometime after they were built, as in the case of the Roxbury meeting house.

While frequently becoming necessary for increased seating capacity, galleries were not inevitably part of the original structure, and there seems to have been no preferred side on which to place a gallery at this period. The earliest meeting house known to have had a gallery eventually was the one at Dorchester, Mass., 1631, to which a "loft" was added in 1634, reached by a stair on the outside.[37] The first meeting house known to have had a gallery built as part of the original plan is more difficult to identify, but it may have been the second one at Hartford, Conn., 1638/39 (*T.R.*, 32).

Little more is known of these first meeting houses until the end of the decade. The meeting house built about 1632 at Lynn, Mass., was said by Edward Johnson to have been "on a levell Land undefended from the cold Northwest wind; and therefore made with steps descending into the Earth."[38] The earliest known dimensions are those of the Dedham, Mass., meeting house, 1638, which was 36 feet long, 20 feet wide, 12 feet high, and thatched (*T.R.*, I, 38). An addition of 25 feet was made to the Salem, Mass., meeting house in 1639 (*T.R.*, 81), but the records are not complete enough to establish the dimensions of either the original or the enlarged building. The first meeting house at Marblehead, Mass., built probably about the same time, was 40 feet long and possibly 22 to 25 feet wide, judging by the dimensions of the meeting house at Hampton, N.H., of 1640, 40 feet long, 22 feet wide, and 13 feet high (*T.R.* 46).[39]

Then a considerably larger building, 50 feet square, was begun in New Haven, Conn., in 1640, built by William Andrews (*T.R.,* 25, 145). At least the town voted that size. Nothing at all comparable in size is known until the Third Church meeting house in Boston of 1669, which was 75 feet long and 51 feet wide.[40] If the first New Haven meeting house was built as intended, it was a large undertaking for those days. At Milford, Conn., in 1640 the meeting house was voted to be 30 feet square, probably a more usual size for that time (*T.R.,* I, 305). Apart from the meeting house at Cambridge, Mass., which was also probably square, the rest of the meeting houses of this period, about which anything at all is known, appear to have been rectangular.

Some of the first meeting houses were probably timber-framed with daubing and thatched roofs, though the records give very little information on this point. The meeting house at Salem, Mass., begun about 1635, was daubed (*T.R.,* 64), and the Dorchester, Mass., meeting house was thatched. The earliest record of clapboards is at Hartford, Conn., October 28, 1640 (*T.R.,* 36). The use of shingles seems to have come later than this period. Flooring is not mentioned directly but may be implied in the "oak and pine boards" ordered for Dedham, Mass., on August 28, 1638 (*T.R.,* I, 48). Some windows were certainly glazed, John Bushnell of Salem, Mass., being paid 7s. 4d. "towards the glassing of windows in the meeting house" on February 15, 1637 (*T.R.,* 64).

The stairs to the "loft" at Dorchester, Mass., have already been mentioned, and a porch with stairs was ordered for the meeting house at Hartford, Conn., in 1640 (*T.R.,* 32). Nothing specific is known about any of the "turrets" mentioned for bells, which rang to summon for meetings or to warn of danger. Some turrets were apparently large enough for a person to enter, as at New Haven, Conn., where a tower was part of the original scheme and where a watchman was to be on the roof at stated times beginning in 1649 (*T.R.,* 485). Others were simply little roofs on posts straddling the ridges or peaks, enough to shelter the bell, with the bell rope hanging down into the building. And contrary to legend, the settlers did not invariably worship in unheated buildings. The contract for the enlargement of the meeting house at Salem, Mass., in 1638 specified "One Catted Chimney of 12 foote longe and 4 foote in height above the top of the building" (*T.R.*, 81). Later at Southampton, N.Y., each family was to "by turn lykewise make a fire in the meeting house upon each Sabathe daye, and to give notice to the next whose turn yt is" (*T.R.*, I, 37).

The interior arrangements of these earliest meeting houses are not known from contemporary description and have been inferred from knowledge of later buildings. At Guilford, Conn., galleries were built on the west and east sides of the 1645 meeting house in 1668 and 1680, and there was a door on the south (*T.R.*, I, 172, 213). This would put the pulpit probably on the north side, where it was most frequently found later. A communion table may have been set prominently before the pulpit, but at this early date it is not certain how regular the furnishings may have been. Thomas Lechford, writing in 1642, described the Lord's Supper with "the Ministers and ruling Elders sitting at the Table, the rest in their seats, or upon forms."[41] Similarly John Cotton described the rite:

> In time of Solemnization of the Supper, the Minister having taken, blessed and broken the bread, and commanded all the people to take and eate it, as the body of Christ broken for them, he taketh it himselfe, and giveth it to all that sit at Table with him, and from the Table it is reached by the Deacons to the people sitting in the next seats about them, the Minister sitting in his place at the Table.[42]

Lechford also described the manner of elections in the Boston meeting house: ". . . all the Freemen are bidden to come in at one doore, and bring their votes in paper, for the new Governour, and Deliver them downe upon the table, before the Court, and so to passe forth at another doore."[43]

Two orders concerning meeting houses appear in the Colony

Records of Massachusetts. One (September 3, 1635) provided that

> hereafter noe dwelling house shall be builte above half a myle from the meeting house, in any newe plantačon, grannted at this Court, or hereafter to be granted, without leave from the Court, (except myll houses and fferme houses of such as have their dwelling houses in some town;) Ipsw^{ch}, Hingham, Neweberry, and Waymothe to be included in this order.[44]

A year later this order was extended "to all the townes in this jurisdiction," and the order was repealed on May 13, 1640.[45]

The other provision was for the designation of meeting houses as watch houses. The Colony Records show this by Court orders for Hingham, Charlestown, Salem, and Lynn in 1639 and 1640.[46]

At Concord, Mass., land was purchased from the Indians on August 5, 1637, according to the deposition of William Buttrick in 1684, "the tract of land being six miles square, the centre being about the place where the meeting-house now stands."[47] After the bargain was concluded, as the deposition of the Christian Indian Jethro, also in 1684, stated: "Mr. Simon Willard, pointing to the four quarters of the world, declared that they had bought three miles from that place, east, west, north, and south; and the said Indians manifested their free consent thereunto."[48]

This description of the position of the meeting house is particularly interesting in the light of the anonymous "Essay on the ordering of towns," written about 1635 and found among the Winthrop Papers, which said: "First. Suppose the Towne square 6 miles euery waye. The Howses orderly placed about the midst, especially the Meetinghouse, the which we will suppose to be the Centor of the wholl Circomference...."[49]

In the *Articles of Agreement* for Londonderry it had been agreed that "the liberties of the Derry and Coleraine shall extend three miles every way."[50] In the case of Londonderry the center of the town was marked not by a church or meeting house but by the fort or watch house.[51] A year earlier than the Concord purchase, the towns of Newton, Watertown, and Charlestown had been ordered to "run eight myles into the country from their meeteing howse."[52] These accounts reflect the importance of the site of the meeting house.

Enough information is available about the Dedham, Mass., meeting house of 1638 that a conjectural sketch may be attempted. (FIGURE 1.) On November 11, 1637,

> Michael Metcalfe, John Luson, Ant⁰ Fisher and Jos: Kingsbury Choesen to contrive the Fabricke of a Meetinghouse to be in length 36 Foote & 20: foote in bredth, & betweene the upp & nether sell in yᵉ studds 12: foote, the same to be girte (*T.R.*, I, 38)

The frame was ready to be raised by May 30, 1638, and the order was given for thatch on August 28. The building was evidently enlarged in 1646 and a turret built for the bell in 1651. Except for the addition of a gallery in 1658, no major changes were made until the decision to build a new meeting house in 1672. (*T.R.*, I, 44, 48, 115, 186; II, 3; III, 4.)

Although the height of the roof is unknown, according to Willsford, the usual proportion of rafter to crossbeam on a thatched building was five to six. Therefore on a building 20 feet wide, the length of the rafter would be 16 feet 8 inches.[53] He also says: "Every thatch'd roof will be deeper from the ridge to the eaves than the rafters are by 3 or 4 feet, caused partly by the thickness of the cover, and for an allowance at the eaves to be cut, and so likewise for the Gable ends."[54] This projection of the thatch is shown, but not the studs and girts, although the building is known to have been daubed (*T.R.*, I, 155).

The number and dimensions of doors and windows are not known. A door 3 feet wide is shown in the center of the long side, and windows are shown between the studs, their length one mentioned by William Leybourn, 2 feet 6 inches.[55] Other arrangements are possible. This one is suggested in order to indicate something of the appearance of the meeting houses in New England of this earliest period.

How these meeting houses were built may at least be surmised, thanks to a few contemporary remarks and surviving town records. Why they were so built is another question. Some help toward the answer may be sought in the late sixteenth- and early seventeenth-century church architecture of Protestant Europe and of England.

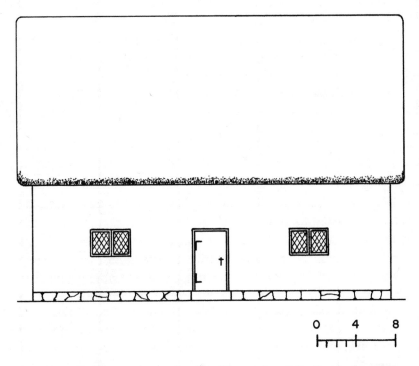

FIGURE 1. Dedham, Mass. Meeting House I. 1638. *Conjectural diagram: Author.*

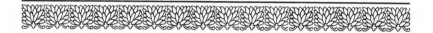

CHAPTER TWO

Continental Protestant Architecture

Before 1630

THE NEW ENGLAND meeting house was one of several developments in religious architecture after the Reformation. Some efforts have been made to identify a specifically "Protestant" ap-
proach to painting and architecture. In the latter case, the term
"Protestant Plain Style" has been devised and applied particularly to the Reformed churches of France and Holland. The New
England meeting houses have been thought to have depended
directly on these Continental churches, partly on architectural
grounds, partly on the grounds of the break that the Congregational churches made with the Established Church in England.[1]

An adequate testing of this hypothesis is not possible at the
present time because no thorough study of Protestant architecture in the sixteenth and early seventeenth centuries has been
made. The major writings of the reformers contain few references
to places of worship, so few in fact that it is questionable whether
Luther, Calvin, and their immediate followers were really interested in church architecture. The greatest amount of early Protestant church building was done in France, primarily after the
Edict of Nantes (1598), and unfortunately nearly all of it was destroyed after the revocation of the Edict of Nantes in 1685. Only
a small number of sketches and descriptions remain. The available information on European Protestant architecture may, however, be summarized in order to indicate the kinds of churches to
which the New England meeting houses were added.

A. *Germany*

A little over a century passed between the beginning of the Reformation in Germany and the settlement of Massachusetts Bay. Yet not until after the Great Migration was there any appreciable Protestant building program in Germany. Prior to the Thirty Years' War, acceptance of Lutheran, and later Genevan, principles of reform varied from one to another of the German territories, unlike the nationwide application of Protestantism in England, and the ravages of war between 1618 and 1648 were hardly favorable to new church building. By the Treaty of Westphalia (October 24, 1648), peace was restored. Although religious toleration was not achieved, the local princes were free to decide whether Lutheranism, Calvinism, or Roman Catholicism would be privileged in their territories.

Up to this time Protestant worship in Germany appears to have been held in the already existing churches, except for a few castle chapels built by Protestant princes. The earliest of these chapels was begun at Torgau by Nikolaus Grohmann for the Elector Johann Friedrich in 1543 and consecrated on October 5, 1544. The chapel was a small "hall church" with galleries in the side aisles, altar at the north end with stairs to the galleries behind it, and pulpit against the middle pier on the east wall.[2] Chapels of this kind were built in Germany before the Reformation, one of the best known being the Castle Chapel at Wittenberg, on the door of which Luther nailed his ninety-five Theses on October 31, 1517.[3] (FIGURE 2.)

Luther himself does not seem to have been much concerned about the planning of churches. Except for what he regarded as objects of false worship, he took a generous view of "all arts, especially music, in the service of Him who has given and created them."[4] He stated his policy concerning the altar in his Preface to the *German Mass and Order of Divine Service* (January 1526):

The Mass vestments, altars and lights may be retained till such time as they shall all change of themselves, or it shall please us to change them: though, if any will take a different course in this

FIGURE 2. Wittenberg, Germany. Castle Chapel. 1490–1509. Drawing of interior. *Courtesy Lutherhalle, Wittenberg.*

matter, we shall not interfere. But in the true Mass, among sincere Christians, the altar should not be retained, and the priest should always turn himself towards the people as, without doubt, Christ did at the Last Supper. That, however, must bide its time.[5]

Nineteen years later, preaching the consecration sermon at Torgau, Luther referred to the building only to say that it should be consecrated not with brush and censer but with prayer and "hearing and expounding God's Word."[6] He then went on to preach from the regular Gospel for the seventeenth Sunday after Trinity, Luke 14: 1–11.

Several other chapels of similar design were built in Germany in the sixteenth century, as at Dresden, 1549–55; Augustusburg, 1568–72; and Schmalkalden, 1587. In the chapel at Wilhelmsburg, 1590, the pulpit was placed above the altar, again an arrangement known before the Reformation.[7] These galleried chapels were well suited for services in which preaching was of great importance, but the Lutherans did not entirely reject the liturgy nor the basic altar-oriented principle of church planning. When Joseph Furttenbach published his proposal for a small Lutheran church in 1649, he repeated the placing of the altar at one end with the pulpit above, reached by steps from the sacristy.[8] The seats were arranged with central and side blocks rather than with a center processional passage. Balancing the sacristy was a square tower with an octagonal belfry and bulbous dome. Classical ornament was carried to lavishness at the altar and pulpit.

Furttenbach's church differed from the castle chapels in that it was a single chamber uninterrupted by piers and therefore more effective as a space in which the entire congregation could see and hear to best advantage. When the Lord's Supper was observed, the communicants left their seats and went forward to the altar to receive the sacrament, men and women separately from their separate places. Here, and in the Lutheran churches of the seventeenth century, the altar remained the focal point of the church, regardless of local variation in details of liturgical practices.[9]

B. *Switzerland and France*

The spread of Protestantism in the early sixteenth century brought differences in liturgical emphasis that were not always defined geographically. Two patterns were set in Switzerland by Zwingli and Calvin. Neither appears to have resulted in new church construction during the first century of the Reformation.

Of the two, Zwingli's rite differed more from the former Mass and from Luther's German Mass. In the *Action oder Bruch des Nachtmals* (Zürich, 1525) instructions were given for the communicants to be seated in the choir and to receive the bread and wine sitting in their places, served by the deacons.[10]

In contrast, the rite published in Geneva by Calvin in 1542 was similar to the German Mass in that the communicants left their places and went forward to the Holy Table to receive the communion. This form of service was followed by the Calvinist churches of France, Holland, and other parts of Europe.[11]

In the Reformed churches of Switzerland, the churches had the consent of civil authority. Consequently in the early years of the Reformation the existing churches were cleared of inappropriate furnishings and adapted for Protestant worship.

In France, on the other hand, the government was essentially committed to Rome, and the French Protestants, or Huguenots, of the sixteenth century enjoyed only brief periods of toleration between long periods of severe persecution. A few places of worship, called "temples," were erected when conditions permitted before a greater toleration was established by the Edict of Nantes. These early French temples have not survived and are known only in part through fragmentary records.

The first French Reformed congregation was organized in Paris in 1565 and the first national synod held in 1559.[12] The Genevan form of worship, already published in 1542 and 1547, was the basis for French Reformed services, held at first in private houses. It has been estimated that by 1561 there were 2,150 Reformed congregations in France, which were mostly private groups in the towns, unlike the congregations of Germany and Switzerland, which were the former parishes.[13] By the Edict of

January 1562, Huguenots were allowed to assemble for worship outside city walls.[14] The war, which broke out soon after, ended in the Pacification of Amboise (March 1563), which restricted Protestant worship to Huguenot towns or to worship outside the walls of one town in each bailiwick.[15]

The next war resulted in the Pacification of St. Germain (1570), containing the important provisions that Reformed worship might be held on the estates of high-ranking noblemen if they, or their families, were present, that the Huguenots might worship where they were already doing so and in two cities of each province, and that the Huguenots were given La Rochelle, Montauban, Cognac, and La Charité for two years as a guarantee of peace.[16] Two years later the massacre of St. Bartholomew's Day, August 24, 1572, opened the next series of wars, which lasted another quarter of a century, until at last an appreciable period of toleration was begun with the Edict of Nantes (April 13, 1598). Then the Huguenots were permitted to worship as in the Pacification of St. Germain, and one additional place was made permissible in each bailiwick. Certain fortified towns, such as La Rochelle, Montauban, and Montpellier, continued in Huguenot hands.[17]

The architectural result of Protestantism in France in the sixteenth century is difficult to assess. Few Huguenot temples could be built under the restrictions of the various edicts or survive the constant wars. The earliest known example appears to have been the so-called "Paradis Temple" in Lyon, built about 1566 and demolished in war almost immediately. This was an oval building, with the pulpit and communion table toward one end and a gallery all the way around.

Three representations of the "Paradis Temple" have survived. The first two are pencil sketches, attributed to Jean Perrissin, now in the Archives Municipales in Lyon.[18] (FIGURES 3 AND 4.) The exterior was apparently quite plain, with round-headed doors, an outside staircase to the gallery, oval windows in the gallery, and dormers in the roof above. The interior was open to the trusses and fitted with benches on all sides facing the pulpit and communion table. The third illustration is a painting of the

FIGURE 3. Lyon, France. "Paradis" Temple. c. 1566. Drawing attributed to Jean Perrissin. *Courtesy Archives Municipales, Lyon.*

FIGURE 4. Lyon, France, "Paradis" Temple. c. 1566. Interior. Drawing attributed to Jean Perrissin. *Courtesy Archives Municipales, Lyon.*

interior, now in the Bibliothèque at Geneva, which has also been attributed to Perrissin, who is said to have been the designer of the building.[19] (FIGURE 5.)

A careful comparison of the two interior views reveals a number of discrepancies in structural details, and it is questionable whether the same artist is responsible for both. The general arrangement is the same in both, however, with the pulpit clearly toward the end of the oval. In the Geneva painting, the pulpit and table are enclosed by a railing, as was to become the practice in Huguenot churches. Both interior views show coats-of-arms in the gallery windows and an elaborate cartouche flanked by inscribed panels on the gallery walls at the pulpit ends. Otherwise, the "Paradis Temple" seems to have had no ornament.

It was not possible for the Huguenots to build many more temples before the Edict of Nantes, and not much is known about the ones that were built. The Temple of Crèvecoeur at Metz, 1576, known through two little sketches by the pastor, Paul Ferry, appears to have been a rectangular building with a gambrel roof and a bell tower at one end, with galleries.[20] The pulpit, a high box with a canopy above, is shown in a sketch of 1654.[21]

Philibert de l'Orme is credited with the design of the Temple at La Rochelle, 1577.[22] This was an octagon, of unequal sides, with three principal doors in the Corinthian Order, an open roof as at Lyon, and benches arranged "en amphithéâtre."[23] The Temple at Montpellier, 1583, was famous for its large vaulted roof[24] and was evidently built of stone, as was the plain rectangular Temple, entered at one side, built at Verteuil in 1583.[25]

Jacques Perret published designs for two temples in his *Des fortifications et artifices* (Paris, 1594). The commentary has been thought to show a Reformed or Calvinist turn of mind,[26] and certainly the designs for a large and small temple provide for rectangular or square buildings with attached towers, interiors without piers, and banks of seats arranged to focus attention on a centralized pulpit.[27]

Following the Edict of Nantes, the French Protestants were able to build temples more freely, but oppressive measures

FIGURE 5. Lyon, France. "Paradis" Temple. c. 1566. Interior. Painting attributed to Jean Perrissin. *Courtesy Bibliothèque, Geneva.*

against the Huguenots were revived in the latter part of the seventeenth century, and nearly all their temples were demolished after the revocation of the Edict in 1685. From what little is known, it would appear that both rectangular and polygonal plans were used, as well as the classical ornamental forms of the French Renaissance.[28] In many Huguenot communities the temple was found in a walled enclosure, which also included the house of the concierge, gardens and orchard, a Consistoire or parish house, a cemetery, and a well, with a dining hall outside the wall for those who came from a distance for all-day sessions. Benches were ranged all around the interior, and a raised parquet, surrounded by a rail, usually stood away from the wall toward one end, on which were placed the communion table, pulpit and reading desk, the pastor's pew, and benches for members of the Consistory.[29] This arrangement differed from that found in the Lutheran churches, but the French Protestants, like the Lutherans, did come forward to the communion table to receive the sacrament, standing or kneeling.

The most famous Huguenot temple, sometimes cited as the prototype or "archetype" of subsequent Protestant churches, was designed in 1623 by Salomon de Brosse for the Paris congregation, meeting at Charenton.[30] De Brosse may have based his design on the basilica at Fano, described by Vitruvius.[31] The Charenton Temple was rectangular, 104 feet long and 66 feet wide, with a double tier of galleries behind columns and balustrades on all sides. (FIGURE 6.) The pulpit enclosure was placed toward one end of the central open area and was surrounded with benches. The pulpit itself appears to have been a high, square structure with canopy. If there were any direct descendants of this temple in France, they have been lost, but it does appear to have inspired the Remonstrant Church at Amsterdam, 1629–30, and also the Synagogue of the Portuguese Jews in the same city.[32]

C. *The Netherlands*

Protestant building began considerably later in the Netherlands than in Germany and France, in spite of the increasing in-

FIGURE 6. Charenton, France. Temple. 1623. Drawing of interior.
Courtesy Kongelige Bibliothek, Copenhagen.

fluence of both Luther and Calvin throughout the sixteenth century. The struggle for independence from Spain dominated these years, until the Truce of 1609 brought some relief, but the final separation did not come until the Treaty of Münster in 1648. Political and religious controversy, closely linked, marred the beginning of a vigorous and creative era in Dutch literature and the arts, science, and commerce. At the Synod of Dort in 1618, the States-General adopted the Calvinist doctrine as official for the Reformed Church in the Netherlands, but no single pattern for Dutch Protestant building resulted.

Like the German and Swiss congregations, the Dutch used their available medieval churches for their new form of worship. Furnishings which were considered offensive were removed from the interiors and high canopied pulpits installed against piers in the central parts of the buildings.[33] The altars sometimes remained in the chancels and the Lord's Supper observed there. In other cases, a communion table was set before the pulpit in a space clear of pews. As with the other Calvinists, the Dutch Reformed worshippers left their pews and went to the altar or communion table to receive the sacrament.

The austerity of these interiors, clearly described in contemporary Dutch paintings, was carried over into new church building activity of the Dutch Renaissance. Several plans were used for the churches built in the first days of Dutch independence. The earliest of these churches, built under Protestant direction, was that at Willemstad, built by Prince Maurice in 1596.[34] This was built as an octagon with steep roof, central turret, and round-headed windows. The pulpit was against one of the side walls, with pews arranged to face it, and also galleries. Classical detail was used throughout, and the whole building may have been inspired by Serlio, since Prince Maurice is known to have been interested in humanistic studies and to have owned some treatises on architecture.[35] A similar church was built at Ijzendike in 1612, though it was less progressive in that pointed windows were retained.[36]

A second type of plan was used by Hendrik de Keyser for the Zuiderkerk in Amsterdam, 1603–11.[37] Here the shell of a basili-

Figure 7. Amsterdam, Holland. Westerkerk. 1620–31. *Photo: Author.*

cal church with nave, aisles, transepts, and tower bears a Gothic shape, transformed by the substitution of classical detail. The interior is simpler, the transepts are not expressed, there is no clearstory, and the nave is covered by a tunnel vault. The altar was omitted and the pulpit placed against the middle pier on one side of the nave. When building the Westerkerk in Amsterdam later, 1620–31, de Keyser added a clearstory, opened out the transepts, and moved the tower from one corner, as in the Zuiderkerk, to project from the west front. (FIGURE 7.) Again the pulpit was set against one pillar of the nave, while a gallery, or mezzanine, occupied the east end.

A third scheme was to use the Greek cross, which could gain additional space on the ground floor by enclosing the triangular spaces between the arms. The church at Blokzijl, 1609–13,[38] lacking the triangular enclosures, appears to be the first cruciform Reformed church in Holland, and it was followed by others, such as the Noorderkerk in Amsterdam, 1620–23,[39] and the church at Maassluis, 1629–30, all these[40] again in the new style of Dutch classicism. (FIGURE 8.) Chancels with altars were no longer provided, and the pulpits were set against piers with surrounding pews.

Generally speaking, in Dutch churches of all types, the space in front of the pulpit was left clear of fixed pews. For the celebration of the Lord's Supper, the communion table was placed before the pulpit, and the communicants came forward from their pews to receive the sacrament.

One of the first Protestant theologians to give extensive attention to the problem of church building was Johann Valentin Andreae (1586–1654). In his ideal city of "Christianopolis," which owed some inspiration to Sir Thomas More, he put the temple in the center of the city. This building, richly decorated, though without "images," was 316 feet in circumference, 70 feet high, and divided into two sections:

> In the one half where the gatherings take place, seats are cut and
> excavated from the earth that the structure may ascend less, and

FIGURE 8. Amsterdam, Holland. Noorderkerk. 1620–23. *Photo: Author.*

that the ears of all may be equally distant on all sides from the voice of the speaker. The other half is reserved for distribution of the sacraments and for music.[41]

The temple was also used for religious drama, and a relation to theater design seems clear. Like Perret's designs for temples, however, it was never adopted for an actual church, and its principal interest remains with the history of utopias.

Until a systematic study of Protestant architecture before 1630 is made available, only general observations are possible. Yet from a brief survey of this period it seems safe to assume that the Continental churches had only limited features in common. The omission of certain liturgical fittings and the appropriate placing of pulpits and communion tables were matters of furnishing that were solved for a variety of church types and sectarian requirements. No single architectural solution was applied to the first needs of Protestant worship in Europe, and there was none to which the earliest New England meeting houses bore a direct structural resemblance.

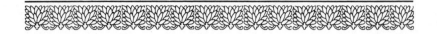

CHAPTER THREE

Reformation to Revolution:
English Worship 1536–1643

To COMPLETE the list of possible sources in Protestant architecture for the New England meeting houses, the effect of the Reformation on Christian worship in England must be taken into account.

Beginning with the first Book of Common Prayer of Edward VI in 1549, the services were conducted in English, the vernacular language. In 1551 the refugee reformer from Strasbourg, Martin Bucer, criticized the retention of the priest's position in the choir, where he read the services, saying that he should be in a central location where all might hear the service.[1] The second Book of Common Prayer of 1552 contained the revised rubric before Mattins that "the morning and evening prayer shall be used in such place of the church, chapel or chancel and the minister shall so turn him as the people may hear."[2]

In the larger churches and cathedrals of England the pulpit was already in the nave, and the issue at stake was not so much hearing the sermons as hearing the words of the various services in the language of the people. The rubric of 1552 gave a flexible instruction whereby each church could rearrange or alter its furnishings according to the needs set by its own size, plan, and proportions. Variety in arrangements resulted, both in existing medieval churches and in the few new ones which were built before the Restoration.

The most controversial piece of church furniture in sixteenth-century England was the altar. The celebration of the Holy Communion could be seen in more than one light, such as a memorial of sacrifice or as a memorial communal meal. The material from which the altar was made and the position it occupied in the church varied according to these possibilities. In the reign of Edward VI, Ridley and Hooper worked to change the stone altars to wooden tables, and, indeed, in 1550 the Privy Council ordered each bishop to have the altars in his diocese removed and wooden tables substituted "in some convenient part of the chancel."[3] The way was now open to move the communion table away from the east wall and set it lengthwise in the middle of the chancel, where the communicants gathered for the celebration of Holy Communion. In many cases the chancel screen was retained, at least the lower portion, to enclose the space reserved for this service.

The brief attempt at restoration of stone altars under Mary I and the resumption of liturgical experiments under Elizabeth I have been recounted elsewhere.[4] Here it may be noted only that the Royal Injunctions of 1559 ordered the communion table to be kept at the east end, where the altar had been, except at the time of Holy Communion. It was then to be moved forward in the chancel "as whereby the minister may be more conveniently heard of the communicants in his prayer and ministration, and the communicants also more conveniently and in more number communicate with the said minister."[5] Soon afterward, in the Interpretations of the Bishops, 1560–61, provision was made for moving the table into the nave "where either the choir seemeth to be too little or at great feasts of receivings."[6] The chancels were furnished with seats, benches, or forms to which the communicants could go at the appropriate moment in the service and at which they knelt to receive the sacrament.

It became customary to leave the table standing out in the chancel or the nave, and in these exposed positions it came to be used simply as a convenient table for parish business or teaching school. At this time English parish churches often had to serve as parish assembly halls, schools, and even markets. Eventually the evident abuse of many communion tables came to distress some

of the clergy, with the move toward reform in this and other matters reaching its height under William Laud, who became Archbishop of Canterbury in 1633. The solution sought was to place
the altar once more at the east end, to set a rail in front of it, run-
ning north-south across the chancel, and to have the communicants receive the sacrament kneeling at the rail. Not all welcomed this arrangement and especially not the Puritans, who
wanted to receive the Holy Communion sitting in their pews.
Many of less Puritanical views also opposed having the altar at
the east end of the chancel because only a few communicants
could crowd into the small medieval chancels and the rest were
unable to see and hear the Altar Prayer of the Communion service. The Laudian program was halted in 1643 when Parliament
issued an ordinance that all altars and tables were to be removed
from the east end and placed in some convenient place in the
chancel or nave.[7]

By the early years of the seventeenth century, a general scheme
for the arrangement of parish churches had been found which
was not affected by varying opinion about the exact locations of
altar and pulpit. This arrangement put the pulpit usually near
the middle of the north or south side of the church, set against
the wall, or against a pier if the church had aisles, and the altar
somewhere toward the east end. In the case of existing medieval
churches with separate chancels, the latter were reserved for
Holy Communion and arranged accordingly. In the case of new
churches or chapels built before the Revolution, the tendency
was to build "auditory" churches, rectangular in plan, with the
chancel now an area, rather than an addition to the nave, set
apart by a screen or raised one step above the main floor.

Of particular interest among late medieval chapels so used are
the records of Blackley Chapel, near Manchester, built sometime
before 1545 and rebuilt in 1736 and 1844.[8] A plan of 1603 is said
to have indicated the pulpit about the middle of the north wall
and the communion table toward the east end with some seats
between it and the wall.[9] This chapel was later served by the Rev.
Thomas Pyke, Presbyterian, who was preaching there in 1668.[10]
Under the Indulgence of 1672 he was licensed to preach at his

house, and of his application for a license to preach in the chapel it was said that it was "on pretence that it was not consecrated and was void of a minister, both of which are false. I suppose in a little time all the chapels, both in Lancashire and Cheshire, may be reckoned unconsecrated places."[11]

Blackley Chapel so described must have been similar to Langley Chapel, near Acton Burnell, Salop., probably built about 1601.[12] Here there is no separate chancel. The altar is on a section raised one step at the east end and was originally surrounded with benches and kneeling desks on three sides. The pulpit is against the south wall just before the altar step, with the reading desk opposite on the north wall.[13] Later, in 1623, the church at Groombridge, Kent, was built according to much the same arrangement: an oblong room without chancel, the pulpit on the south, the altar raised three steps at the east end, with a south porch and a flat bell turret on the west end.[14]

These English churches and chapels, and the others built before the Puritan Revolution, were built for worship in the church of England, as established in 1559. Dissension rose early, the two parties who figured in the settlement of New England being the Separatists and the Puritans. Neither was able to build places of worship before the Revolution of 1642, and they had no uniquely Separatist or Puritan type of church to transfer to the New World. Both parties met secretly in private houses in the late sixteenth and early seventeenth centuries, as the Independents were to do again after the Restoration.

The Separatists, or Brownists, made a definite break with the Church of England, asserting the independence of each congregation that Robert Brown described in his *A treatise of reformation without tarrying for any* (1582). Brown himself returned to the Anglican church in 1586. Repression of dissent was strong in England at this time, culminating in the Act against Puritans of 1593.[15] The London Separatists, who had continued their fellowship after Brown's recantation, eventually went to Amsterdam, with Francis Johnson as their pastor and Henry Ainsworth as their teacher.

Permission for the Separatists to settle in Amsterdam was granted reluctantly by the Dutch authorities, with whom the Separatists were never fully in sympathy. Francis Johnson's *Articles against the French and Dutch* (1601) listed ten differences between the Separatists and the Calvinists, including that the latter met in existing churches that had been used for Roman Catholic worship, where "the anti-Christian stones have some of them the ornaments of the Roman Harlot upon them remaining."[16] The French Reformed had had but three years of tolerance since the Edict of Nantes, and the Dutch had not yet signed the Twelve Years' Truce with Spain (1609), making it unlikely that either could have built many new churches by 1601. The Separatists would not regard these circumstances as excusing the use of former Roman Catholic structures, since they were long accustomed to worshipping in private houses. In their *Confession* (1596) they went further, stating in Article 39: "That it is the Office and duty of Princes and Magestrates . . . to abolish and destroy the Idoll Temples, Images, Altares, Vestments, and all other monuments of Idolatrie and superstition."[17]

On the accession of James I in 1603, the Separatists added a supplementary petition to the *Millenary Petition* of the Puritans. Article XII requested

> . . . that all monuments of idolatry in garments or any other things, all Temples, Altars, Chappels, and other places dedicated heertofore by the Heathens or Antichristians to their false worship, ought by lawfull authoritie to be rased and abolished, not suffered to remayne, for nourishing superstition, much lesse imploied to the true worship of God.[18]

Henry Ainsworth furnished Scriptural authority for such a view in his statement to Hugh Broughton in 1605:

> I refer you to the scripture, which condemneth the antichristian worship, for idolatrie and worship of divils, and maketh Babylon the habitation of divils; and hath forbidden us all manner of communion and fellowship with divils or idols; or retayning and using any monuments of their abomination . . . .[19]

40

Francis Johnson repeated these sentiments in 1617, asking in *A Christian plea* "whether it be not the dutie of the Magistrate, to take away and demolish all remnants and monuments of Idolatrie and superstition, Images, Altars, Temples, garments and the like, with all maner of false worship whatsoever."[20]

On February 4, 1607, the Separatists, led by Johnson and Ainsworth, are recorded as having applied to friends in England and having

> obtained money to build a house to dwell in and to preach in secretly, if need be. But soon after, on March 16, 1607, the beforesaid Brownist preaching-house being half-ready, God sent his strong wind most furiously from heavens and cast the house only, and no other, flat down in to the ground, which was a sign that they do not build upon the rock, the true and wise foundation.[21]

The Separatists had been meeting in Francis Johnson's house, where he had lived in 1597[22] and where he apparently continued to live until a quarrel split the congregation in 1610. The group siding with Ainsworth moved to a neighboring house, returning to the original house when the group siding with Johnson moved to Emden in 1612.[23]

In England the Separatists continued to meet secretly in private houses: "They doe not flocke all together, but come 2 or 3 in a company . . . and all being gathered together, the man appointed to teach stands in the midst of the Roome, and his audience gather about him."[24] Apparently large numbers gathered in some houses, for we read of such episodes as the following: "One Burboone, a Letherseller, entertained a whole swarme of Brownists (as by credible information the number of one hundred and fifty)."[25]

The Separatists, as this summary of their history would indicate, for all their abhorrence of "idol Houses," never grew to enough strength or harmony to develop a building program appropriate to their manner of worship.

The Puritans, on the other hand, did not at first intend to separate from the Church of England but rather to reform it more stringently. Neither Elizabeth I nor James I was prepared to tolerate a faction that wished to abolish the episcopacy and denied that the monarch was the Supreme Head of the Church in England. Puritan opposition to the use of ceremonies and vestments for which they found no scriptural authority did not extend to their existing church buildings. In these they were content to worship according to their own views, and their departures from the rule of the Book of Common Prayer are reflected in numerous Visitation Articles. Probably the usage most closely allied with the church architecture or furnishing was that of receiving the sacrament sitting, on which they insisted in their first open statement, the *Admonition to the Parliament* (1572): "They [the first Christians] receaved it (Matt. 26:20; Mark 14:18; Luke 22:14; John 13:28) sitting . . . we pompously, with singing, pyping, surplisse and cape wearyng."[26]

Measures taken against the Puritans failed to suppress their activities, which were carried on in conventicles or meetings in private houses, barns, or even open fields. The Act against Puritans (1593) forbade that anyone should "willingly join, or be present at, any such assemblies, conventicles, or meetings, under colour or pretence of any such exercise of religion, contrary to the laws and statutes of this realm."[27]

In the Visitation Articles for London under Archbishop Bancroft for the year 1605, the bishop is enjoined to inquire

> whether both your minister, or any other person or persons within your parish, used to meet in any private house or other place, there to consult together, how to impeach or deprave the Book of Common Prayer, or the doctrine or discipline of the Church of England.[28]

Similarly, in the provinces, the Visitation Articles of Bishop John Thornborough at Bristol asked in 1603

> whether your parson, vicar or minister doth at anytime minister the Communion or Sacraments of the Lord's Supper, to any his parishioners or other, sitting or standing, but always humbly kneeling; and not in their several seats, where they usually sit in

the church, but kneeling in the seats severally appointed in your several churches for the communicants, to receive the same.[29]

Before the Great Migration to New England, Separatists and Puritans alike rejected the continued observance of ceremonies for which they did not find scriptural authority and worshipped in private houses if necessary. Plymouth, the earlier colony, was settled by another group of Separatists who had organized first at Scrooby in the house of William Brewster and had migrated to New England via Amsterdam and Leiden. The Plymouth colonists took with them no ideas about places of worship except the rejection of the parish church, and they did not build a separate meeting house until 1648. But the Puritan ministers preached in their parish churches in England when they could, and it was they who settled Massachusetts Bay in the 1630's and who built the first New England meeting houses.

CHAPTER FOUR

Meeting Houses of the
Middle Period: 1643–1660

Events of 1643 climaxed periods of development in England and New England and formed marking points from which the middle years of the century may be viewed conveniently. In England the Long Parliament passed an Act to Abolish the Episcopacy, and the Westminster Assembly set the pattern for a Presbyterian form of worship and church government that was to be followed in England during the Commonwealth, 1649–60.

Meanwhile, also in 1643, the Massachusetts Bay, Plymouth, Connecticut, and New Haven colonies formed the New England Confederation, a gesture, at least, toward a more formal unity after the first rush of settlement. The period before the Restoration was thus the time of greatest strength of the original Puritan experiment in New England and also a time when its influence was strongly felt in England. During the Civil War and Commonwealth few new settlers arrived in New England, and, in fact, a sizable group returned to England, including some ministers who had studied at Harvard.

Available records indicate that forty-one more meeting houses were built between 1643 and 1660. Of these twenty-nine were for new congregations and twelve replaced older structures now too small or fallen into disrepair. Twenty-seven were built in Massachusetts, six in Connecticut, four on Long Island, three in New Hampshire, and one in Maine. The records are somewhat more extensive than for the earlier years and provide a few more details about the buildings.

44

As in the first years of settlement, worship in new communities was held in private houses.[1] At Easthampton, L.I., the meetings prior to 1652 were held at Thomas Baker's house (*T.R.*, I, 19), and at Middletown, Conn., also prior to 1652, at John Gale's house (*T.R.*, 10). The names of a few builders are known: John Rutter (Sudbury, Mass., 1643), George Norton (Ipswich, Mass., 1646), Thomas Davis (Haverhill, Mass., 1647), Richard Waldern (Dover, N.H., 1652), Thomas Plympton and Peter King (Sudbury, Mass., 1653), Valentine Hill (Oyster River, N.H., 1656), John Sherman (Watertown, Mass., 1656), and Job Lane (Malden, Mass., 1658). Dimensions are recorded for twelve of these buildings, of which five were square and seven rectangular,[2] and enough details are known of four other meeting houses to make it fairly certain that they were rectangular.

Many of these meeting houses were built and furnished piecemeal, with bell turrets, galleries, and additional seats provided some years after the first construction. Neither turrets nor galleries were necessarily part of the original plan of a meeting house. The bell was, in fact, sometimes supported on a frame entirely apart from the building, as at Medfield, Mass. (*T.R.*, 92), and Dorchester, Mass. (*T.R.*, 236), an arrangement recalling the occasional use of separate bell towers in England. The turrets built on square meeting houses, such as the one at Cambridge, Mass., 1650, were probably always built in the middle of a hipped roof, as is shown in eyewitness sketches of a few of the later meeting houses.[3] No location is given for any of the turrets built on rectangular meeting houses of this period. The vote at Springfield, Mass., in 1644 to build two turrets, one for a bell and one for a watch house, suggests one at each end, with the building measuring 40 feet by 25 feet (*T.R.*, I, 37). These turrets on the rectangular meeting houses may have been like the bell-cotes on frame churches in England, such as Besford Church, Worcs., at the west end of the building, supported on a tie beam of the roof.[4]

In view of the alleged dependence of New England meeting houses on the Temple at Charenton with its tiers of galleries, the use of galleries in New England in these first two periods is particularly interesting. At least eighty meeting houses were built in New England by 1660. Sixteen of them are known to have had galleries.[5] Four (Dorchester, Ipswich, Medfield, and Newbury, Mass.) may have had these galleries from the beginning, but the records are not decisive. The other galleries were added several years after the original construction, not always on all sides of the building at the same time, and there appears to have been no fixed policy regarding the inclusion of galleries in the meeting houses.

A few other details may be noted for this middle period, such as the shutters made for the windows of the Dorchester, Mass., meeting house in 1662/63 (*T.R.,* 112). The seats of the Wethersfield, Conn., meeting house were to be with wainscot, like those in Hartford, Conn., in 1647 (*T.R.,* April 1647). A most curious statement remains that the Norwalk, Conn., meeting house of 1657 was "to be set upon posts" (*T.R.,* 29), apparently in the manner of English market halls. This is the only instance of this kind of construction suggested by town records known at present.

Tentative plans or elevations may be attempted when the records furnish a comparatively generous amount of information. No certainty can be claimed for the details of the conjectural diagrams. They have been composed from the known facts about each building and from reference to contemporary English building methods as seen in extant buildings and printed sources.

At Sudbury, Mass., on February 17, 1642/43, the town voted that John Rutter should build a meeting house

> thirty foote longe twenty foote wide eight foot be . . . ioynte three footte betweene studde two crosse Dorments in . . . house six clearstory windowes two with foure light a peece and foure with three lights a peece and to entertise between ye studde . . . . (*T.R.,* 43)

FIGURE 9 gives one possible elevation for this building. Length and height are known. The roofing material is not specified, and thatch has been assumed in giving the roof a 50° pitch, steeper than would have been necessary for shingle. If the studs were centered 3 feet apart, starting at the center of a 12-inch corner post, a 4-foot interval comes in the middle, in which a door might be conveniently framed, as indicated in the drawing. The same setting of studs would provide for the framing of the two four-light windows, one on either side of the door, taking up two bays, and set above the girt.

"Clearstory" windows are defined by Moxon as "windows that have no Transum in them," i.e., plain casement windows.[6] A previous restoration drawing indicated clapboards,[7] which have been omitted here since there is no documentary evidence for them. To "entertise" meant to set horizontal binding members between the studs,[8] and a "dorment" was a "great Beam lying cross a house."[9] If the arrangement of the door and four-light windows that is assumed here is correct, the four three-light windows could have been set easily between the studs on the ends and the back. The centrally located door would also place the next set of studs directly beneath the "dorments," if the latter were laid as was customary about 10 feet apart. An arrangement with the door toward one end of the meeting house would produce a less symmetrical design for the whole frame, but must not be ruled out as a possibility in the absence of further records.

The first Sudbury meeting house is nevertheless one of the best-documented of the smaller buildings, which included the Dedham, Mass., meeting house of 1638 (Figure 1, above) and those of Southampton, L.I., 1651 (30 feet by 24 feet); Easthampton, L.I., 1652 (26 feet by 20 feet); and Norwalk, Conn., 1657 (30 feet by 18 feet).

The first meeting house at Springfield, Mass., begun two years after the Sudbury meeting house, was larger and more elaborate. On February 28, 1644/45, Thomas Cooper was instructed to

> build the house in length 40 foote, in breadth 25 foote, 9 foote be-twixt joynts, double studded, 4 large windows, two on each side, and one smaller windowe at each end, one large doore at the south side, and two smaller doors as shall be thought convenient; to lay justs for a floore above, to shingle the roofe, with two turrets for a bell and a watch house, to underpin the house with stoane, to daube the wales, to provide glass for the windows (if the pay he hath of the Plantation will procure it) alsoe to find nayles and iron workes for the ful completing of the buildinge, which is to be finished by the 30th September, 1646. (*T.R.*, I, 37)

47

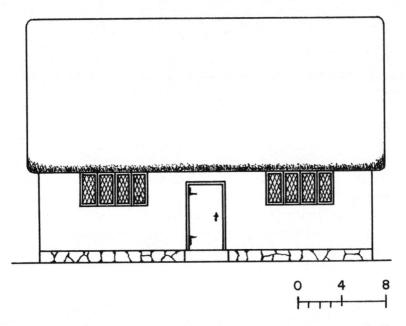

FIGURE 9. Sudbury, Mass. Meeting House I. 1643. *Conjectural diagram: Author.*

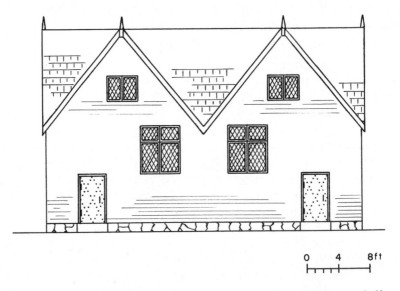

FIGURE 10. Sudbury, Mass. Meeting House II. 1653. *Conjectural diagram: Author.*

There was an "Alley" with a door at the end (*T.R.*, I, 357), but again it is not possible to say whether it ran lengthwise or cross-wise.

The second Sudbury meeting house, 1653, provides an additional example to that of Springfield of the larger rectangular meeting houses, and again it may be suggested by a sketch. (FIG-URE 10.) On November 27, 1652, Thomas Plympton and Peter King were voted to build a meeting house

> 40 foote longe and twe . . . wide, measuring from outside to outside twelve foote be . . . yᵉ studde 6 inches & 4 & to stand for a 4 foote clapboard to . . . there is to bee 4 transom windows 5 foote wide & 6 foote . . . of them in yᵉ foreside & one at each end 2 gable ends . . . yᵉ foreside to answere yᵉ height & leingth of yᵉ house . . . & pinacles both at each end & each gable wth a clear story . . . each end & in each gable each window 4 foote wide & 3 foote . . . sufficient Dorments a cross yᵉ house fitt for galleries if yᵉ hath a desire afterwards to sett up gallerys . . . to make 2 do . . . 3 foote & a halfe wide nayled Diamond fashion yᵉ house is to . . . purlyned 2 beames & across yᵉ house to be brased at each end . . . by 10 inches & 14 yᵉ groundsills are to be white oake & . . . yᵉ plates are to be 8 ynches square yᵉ posts a foote square . . . & yᵉ 2 middle beames to be smothed on three sides & yᵉ lower . . . to be run with a bowkell . . . they are to inclose yᵉ house with claborde to daube it . . . to lyne yᵉ inside with Cedar or otherwise with good spruce. . . . (*T.R.*, 293)

Since the records state that the studs were "to stand for a 4 foote clapboard," a number divisible by 4 has been chosen for the width of the meeting house, 24 feet. This is similar to the widths of other 40-foot-long meeting houses, such as those in Springfield, Mass. (25 feet wide) and Dover, N.H. (26 feet wide).

Although the covering of the roof is unknown, this new and larger meeting house was probably finished with shingle rather than thatch. According to Willsford, the most common proportion for length of rafter to length of beam for a shingled roof is 3 to 4,[10] which is the "true pitch" defined by the *Builder's Dictionary*.[11] This proportion gives rafters 18 feet long for a building 24 feet wide and is the basis for the height of the roof as shown in

Figure 10. The size and placement of the gables on the front are then easily determined since they were to "answere yᵉ height & leingth of yᵉ house."

Placing the doors and windows is not quite so automatic, but the records furnish some guide. If the studs were set 4 feet apart to accommodate the clapboards, a center door would interrupt the center stud. It would also make an opening directly beneath the junction of the two gables, making it impossible to put a strong support at this point. The records direct Plympton and King to "make 2 do . . . 3 foote & a halfe wide." Doors 3 feet 6 inches wide with their casings could be placed between studs 4 feet apart and have been drawn in this manner.

Four "transom" windows are specified, 5 feet high and 6 feet wide, two on the front and one on each end. A transom window was one in which the casement was divided by a wooden strip.[12] At Derby, Conn., the transom windows ordered in 1681 were to have "3 lights in each tere afott & ahalf in length in yᵉ loer Length; & afott in yᵉ upper tere" (*T.R.,* 122). In Figure 10 the transom strip is placed toward the top as suggested by the records at Derby. In each gable a "clear story" window, without transom, is shown, 4 feet wide and 3 feet high.

The pinnacles indicated on the gables are recorded for several other meeting houses, usually as "pyramids": Dedham, Mass. (*T.R.,* 1636–59, 196); Boston, Mass., Third Church (Figure 18 below); Haddam, Conn. (*T.R.,* 35); New London, Conn. (*T.R.,* 191); Norwich, Conn. (*T.R.,* Kelly II, 110); and Simsbury, Conn. (*T.R.,* 32). Such "pyramids" occasionally appear in contemporary English literature as symbolic devices, but on the meeting houses they appear to have been only a survival of medieval ornamental forms.[13]

Similar dimensions were specified for the Dover, N.H., meeting house of 1652: "The Dementions of the said house is to be forty foote long twenty six foote side sixteene foot stud with six windows two doores sett for such a house" (*T.R.,* 262). The builder was Richard Waldern. Nothing is known about the roof except that a turret for the bell was added in 1666.[14] The placement of doors and windows is not described but may have been like that suggested for Sudbury. These three meeting houses, Springfield, Sudbury, and Dover, continue the general size and type of building which, if not established at Hampton, N.H., in 1640, is at least first recorded there.

A third kind of meeting house was the square building with hip roof and turret, first known at New Haven, Conn., in 1640. Similar meeting houses, 40 feet square, were built at Cambridge, Mass., 1650; Watertown, Mass., 1656; and Portsmouth, N.H., 1657. Smaller square meeting houses were built at Middletown, Conn., 1653 (20 feet square), and Malden, Mass., 1658 (33 feet square).

The contract for the Malden meeting house had a plan drawn on the back and was extant in 1850 when the text was published.[15] Unfortunately it has since been lost. A plan drawn from that on the back of the contract was included in the 1850 publication and is reproduced here (FIGURE 11), together with its accompanying elevation (FIGURE 12). FIGURE 13 is the elevation redrawn to scale for comparison and correction. The door has been widened and drawn six feet high, and the heads of the windows are shown set into the intermediate girts as specified in the contract. The two windows "on each side of the desk" in the second story have not been drawn directly above the first floor windows but have been placed closer to the center of the building, where they would light the pulpit more effectively.

The roof of the Malden meeting house is shown in Figure 13 with a railed platform and turret, a more probable construction than the one suggested by the 1850 drawing. The pitch chosen here is "true pitch," drawn according to John Browne's instructions for constructing a hip roof with true pitch.[16] The turret was specified to be 6 feet square, and the platform as shown would extend about 3 feet on all sides. The other meeting houses reported to have had hip roofs with turrets were probably similar.

From the amount of information available from town records up to 1660, it may be fairly concluded that three general types of meeting houses were in use by then, all apparently known from the early years of settlement and none, according to present evidence, particularly favored.

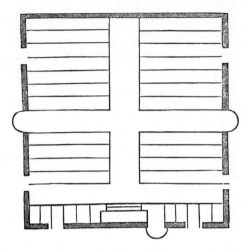

FIGURE 11. Malden, Mass. Meeting House II. 1658. Plan. *Bi-Centennial Book of Malden*, p. 126. *Courtesy Harvard College Library.*

FIGURE 12. Malden, Mass. Meeting House II. 1658. Elevation. *Bi-Centennial Book of Malden*, p. 126. *Courtesy Harvard College Library.*

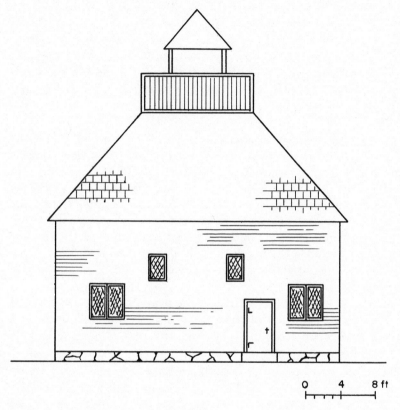

FIGURE 13. Malden, Mass. Meeting House II. 1658. *Conjectural diagram: Author.*

While the new towns were being settled and new meeting houses constructed in New England between 1643 and 1660, a different set of circumstances was affecting the worship of the Puritans remaining in England.

Opposition to the Established Church at home came from both Puritans and Presbyterians, who agreed on some issues and disagreed on others. Charles I was forced to summon the Long Parliament, as it became known, in November 1640. Less than a year later the Commons declared

> that the Church-wardens of every Parish Church and Chapel respectively, do forthwith remove the Communion-Table from the East End of the Church, Chapel, or Chancel, into some other convenient Place; and that they take away the Rails, and level the Chancels, as heretofore they were before the late Innovations; that all Crucifixes, scandalous Pictures of any one or more Persons of the Trinity, and all Images of the Virgin Mary, shall be taken away and abolished, and that all Tapers, Candelsticks, and Basons, be removed from the Communion-Table.[17]

The Civil War broke out soon after, in August 1642. Support for the King came mainly from rural areas, which had been little affected by rising commerce and manufacturing. Support for the Parliamentary party came from London, the seaports, the manufacturing districts, and East Anglia, which had long been a region of lively Puritan activity. By 1643 Parliament found it necessary to call upon the Scots for military assistance and, in order to secure it, had to agree to the Solemn League and Covenant. The acceptance of a Presbyterian form of church government did not carry with it any general toleration. As the Westminster Assembly convened and set about preparing a directory for public worship, the Presbyterians were not receptive to the ideas of the Puritans, who were now being called Independents or Congregationalists.

Even before the actual outbreak of the Civil War, some of the New England adventurers were rejoining their friends in England. In 1641 John Winthrop wrote that the hope of reformation of church and state "caused all men to stay in England in expectation of a new world," and the pastors Hugh Peters of Salem,

Thomas Wilde of Roxbury, and William Hibbins of Boston went back "to congratulate the happy success there . . . and . . . to give any advice, as it should be required, for the settling the right form of church discipline there."[18]

This advice was not universally welcomed in England, partly because the Independents did not favor church government by synods. The issue of differences in worship was brought out sharply in the Westminster Assembly over the question of the communion table. The exasperation the Independents caused to the Presbyterians is reflected in a series of letters sent back to Scotland by Robert Baillie in 1644. In one dated April 2, 1644, Baillie said:

> We agreed, so far as we went, except in a table. Here all of them opposeth us, and we them. They will not, and saith the people will never yield to alter their practice. They are content of sitting, albeit not as of a ryte institute, but to come out of their pews to a table, they deny the necessitie of it: we affirme if necessare, and will stand to it.[19]

Baillie reported the Independent position again in June of the same year:

> We are proceeding in our Assemblie. This day before noone we gott sundrie propositions of our Directory for the Sacrament of the Lord's Supper past; but in the afternoone we could not move one inch. The unhappie Independents would mangle that sacrament. No catechising nor preparation before; no thanksgiving after; no sacramental doctrine, or chapters, in the day of celebration; no coming up to any table; but a carrying of the element to all in their seats athort the church: yet all this, with God's help, we have carried over their bellies to our practise.[20]

Yet another complaint was made August 7, 1644: "We hope God will provide remeeds for that evill of Independency, the mother and true foundation of all the church distractions here."[21] These comments confirm Lechford's description of the Congregational mode of worship.

In spite of interruptions from the Independents, Parliament did abolish the Book of Common Prayer and accept the Westminster Directory on January 3, 1644/45 (*L.J.* vii, 121–22; *C.J.* iv, 9).[22] The Act against Episcopacy had already passed Parliament on January 26, 1942/43 (*C.J.* ii, 948). The first legislation for a Presbyterian form of church government was enacted August 5, 1645, in the Directions for the Election of Elders (*L.J.* vii, 544–45; *C.J.* iv, 242), and again, on June 9, 1646, Parliament ordered the establishment of Presbyterianism (*C.J.* iv, 569).

This triumph of the Presbyterians in Parliament did not last. They began secret negotiations with the king in February 1646/47, which were followed soon after by the alliance of the Independents with the Army, the second phase of the Civil War, and the eventual success of the Army. By the purge of December 1648, Parliament was reduced to about sixty Independents, who abolished the House of Lords and declared England a Commonwealth. In only four years, then, after the acceptance of the Westminster Directory, England was again torn by war, and the civil authority was taken over by the Independents.

The Presbyterian system, which was never annulled by the Independents, was not well enforced, either in London or the provinces. Scottish Presbyterianism had not been sought but had been imposed on the English by the Solemn League and Covenant, and by the later 1640's was viewed with hostility or indifference. The new Parliament in its turn, having failed to bring about orderly government and having stirred up resentment by attempting to enforce strict Puritan standards of conduct, was ejected by the Army in 1653. The succeeding Parliaments under the Protectorate attempted no further innovations in church affairs, and the next major change came with the restoration of the Anglican Church in 1660.

The foregoing outline of ecclesiastical history in England between 1643 and 1660 indicates the contrast of the Puritan position in England with that in New England. The New England Puritans were comparatively well organized and in control throughout this period. The English Puritans were organized primarily through Oliver Cromwell's Army and were opposed by Anglicans and Presbyterians. No extensive new building programs were possible in these years. The existing parish churches continued in use, with the provision of the Westminster Directory that

As no place is capable of any holiness, under pretence of what-soever dedication or consecration, so neither is it subject to such pollution by any superstition formerly used, and now laid aside, as may render it unlawful or inconvenient for Christians to meet together therein for the Public Worship of God. And therefore we hold it requisite, that the places of public assembling for worship among us should be continued and employed to that use.[23]

Some of the churches and chapels that were built during the Civil War and the Commonwealth have been destroyed or extensively rebuilt. Those that survive with little change appear to be Anglican in their present arrangement, regardless of the persuasion of the ministers who once preached in them.

In the latter category are churches at Berwick-on-Tweed, Northum., 1648–52; Great Houghton, Yorks., about 1650; Staunton Harold, Leics., 1653; Brampton Bryan, Heres., 1656; and St. Ninian's at Brougham, Westm., 1660.

With or without structural chancels and aisles, these churches were fitted with altars behind rails and the pulpit part-way down one side. The churches at Staunton Harold and Brougham were apparently used by Anglican rectors only. In 1662 the rectors of Brampton Bryan, Berwick-on-Tweed, and Great Houghton were ejected for Nonconformity, either as Congregational or Presbyterian.[24] These men probably had no altar rails in their time, though the rails are present now. A similar situation seems to have occurred at Chewbent, Lancs., where a chapel was built by John Atherton in 1645, not consecrated until 1723, and replaced 1814.[25] Atherton built the chancel and his tenants the body of the church, which was, however, used for Presbyterian worship until 1717. The chapels at Elswick, Lancs., about 1646–50, and Sankey, Lancs., before 1650, were also built as chapels-of-ease and used for Presbyterian worship, but they have both disappeared.[26]

A chapel frequently cited as an early example of Puritan architecture is the one on the manor of Bramhope, Yorks., built in 1650 by Robert Dyneley.[27] (FIGURE 14.) The building is long and narrow, with two entrances on the south side. It was formerly furnished with box pews, a pulpit in the center of the north side, and a communion table at the east end behind a modern gate.

FIGURE 14. Bramhope, Yorks. Dyneley Chapel. 1650. *Photo: Author.*

The plain panelling of the pulpit (now in the Abbey House Museum, Kirkstall, Leeds), together with its location, has suggested a Puritan design to some observers. The panelling, however, appears stylistically later in date than 1650.[28] and it must be further noted that the chapel was built not for Puritan but for Presbyterian worship. On January 9, 1650, the land was deeded to Dyneley, fourteen freeholders, and Robert Todd, rector of St. John's, Leeds, who introduced Presbyterianism there.[29] The minister of the chapel was Jeremiah Crossley, whose persuasion is not recorded, but who was visited there by the great Presbyterian preacher Oliver Heywood on November 5, 1664.[30] If the known fittings were the original ones, the placing of the communion table at the east end would have been appropriate for Presbyterian worship, though the chapel is so narrow that any observance of the Lord's Supper would have been crowded. The narrowness is in itself contrary to the proportions of Puritan or Independent chapels built later, and the exterior is plain late Gothic, with arched mullioned windows and a bell-cote at the west end.

Another private chapel used for Presbyterian worship was built at Ellenthorpe, Yorks., by Lady Brooke in 1656.[31] (FIGURE 15.) This was built with the minister's quarters above the chapel. The combination of chapel and residence may be seen in other examples, such as St. Mary's at Great Horkesley, Essex[32] (FIGURE 16), and the Black Chapel at North End, Essex,[33] both dating from the fifteenth century. The chapel at Ellenthorpe is no longer used for services.

Of the churches and chapels built in England during the Civil War and Commonwealth, none can be shown to have been designed according to unquestionably "Puritan" principles. Three further chapels are alleged to have been so built, the Baptist Chapel at Stony Stratford West, Bucks.; the Chapel at Peckham, Surrey; and the Baptist Chapel at Cote, Oxon. The first has been entirely rebuilt, but a late seventeenth-century window frame remains to suggest that the congregation, though founded in 1656, did not build until later in the century. The minister was licensed to preach in his house in 1672.[34] At Peckham, the record of the chapel in 1657 is hearsay, and a chapel is not mentioned in the

FIGURE 15. Ellenthorpe, Yorks. Chapel. 1656. *Photo: Author.*

FIGURE 16. Great Horkesley, Essex. Chapel of St. Mary. 15th Century. *Photo: Courtesy National Monuments Record.*

records of conventicles in 1669 or licenses of 1672.[35] The Baptist congregation at Cote appears to have been founded in 1657. The minister was licensed at his house in 1672, however, and the building appears to belong more toward the end of the century.[36] (FIGURE 17.)

The structural and documentary remains of these churches do not reveal any specifically Puritan movement in English architecture that could have contributed to the development of meeting houses in New England. There are, on the other hand, a few indications of New England influence upon England before the Restoration. Winthrop's comments about the return of settlers to England have already been noted, and at least thirty-three ministers returned to England before 1660, all but one of whom had emigrated to New England by 1640. All these men were later ejected from their parishes for Nonconformity in 1662. Winthrop said in 1645 that "the scarcity of good ministers in England, and want of employment for our new graduates here, occasioned some of them to look abroad."[37] It has not yet been possible to connect any of these men with the construction of an Independent church in England, but a few remarks in contemporary documents suggest their possible impact on English congregations.

Nathaniel Mather, who had gone to New England in 1635 with his father, Richard, and brother Samuel, was back in London by March 1651, whence he wrote his friend John Rogers at Ipswich, Mass.: ". . . the naked truth is, here is a great incouragement for any to come over . . . for it is with the honestest on both sides a matter of high account to have been a New English man."[38] Mather made similar comments in a letter of December 23, 1651: "It is incredible what an advantage to preferment it is to have been a New English man."[39]

A few years later, Richard Byfield, minister of Long Ditton, Surrey, and "6 Godly inhabitants" petitioned the Protector and Council for permission to rebuild their dilapidated church "and see that the church is not built in the old superstitious way of chancel, church and church porch, but in one entire room."[40]

FIGURE 17. Cote, Oxon. Baptist Chapel. Late 17th Century. *Photo: Courtesy National Monuments Record.*

This petition was not granted, and the church, now again in ruins, was eventually rebuilt on its medieval foundations.[41]

Even more interesting is the petition of the "Congregational or gathered church" of Bury St. Edmunds, Suffolk, on November 4, 1658. Stating that "we have met in an obscure way, and in a place hazarding our lives through cold in the winter," and that the Presbyterians "enjoy both the parish meeting places," they ask for one of the "meeting-places":

> If this be not thought meet, we beg that the chancel of St. Mary's parish, which is now a mere superfluity, may be parted from the body of the meeting house, the place being so large that 2 congregations can meet without disturbing each other.[42]

No earlier use of the term "meeting house" has been found in England with reference to a religious building, regardless of sect. Interestingly enough it is here used by a Congregational church and applied to an existing, consecrated, medieval building.

Among the Independent churches New England evidently enjoyed considerable prestige in the 1650's, and there are these few indications that accounts of meeting houses in New England may have begun to exert a little influence in the mother country. Certainly by 1660 neither the Independents nor the Presbyterians had developed a building program such as was flourishing in New England.

CHAPTER FIVE

Meeting Houses of the Late Period: 1661–1700

ALTHOUGH by 1661 New England meeting houses were being built in increasing numbers, the fortunes of the original Bible State were beginning to decline. Already in 1657 the Half-Way Covenant had made possible the baptism of children whose baptized parents were not yet church members. This measure reflected the views of the second and third generations, who lacked the fervor of their parents and grandparents. The growth of the colonies, which resulted in many more "second" meeting houses, brought the more worldly standards denounced by Michael Wigglesworth in 1662. *An Exhortation unto reformation* by Samuel Torrey (1674) and the *Necessity of reformation* published by the Synod of 1679 further testify to the more conservative Puritans' distress over what they saw as a moral decline.

Not only were the clergy unable to enforce the original Puritan standards of conduct, they were also unable to maintain political control. In 1662 the Connecticut and New Haven colonies were united under a royal charter, and Massachusetts was ordered to extend the franchise outside the Congregational Church. The Charter of the Massachusetts Bay Company was revoked in 1684 and Sir Edmond Andros made Governor, who was replaced by Sir William Phips in 1691.[1]

Growth in size and prosperity of the New England towns was reflected in the number of meeting houses built and in the size of some of them. Between 1661 and 1700 one hundred twenty-two meeting houses were built, of which fifty-two were new, fifty-eight were the second buildings on their sites, eleven were the third, and one was the fourth. Seventy were built in Massachusetts, thirty-seven in Connecticut, five in Maine, five on Long Island, three in New Hampshire and two in Rhode Island, the Long Island towns being at that time linked with Connecticut. Known dimensions or other details indicate that thirty-nine (and possibly six more) were rectangular in plan, while fourteen (and possibly one more) were square.

As with the earlier meeting houses, individual details of construction are known for a number of the buildings, but extensive descriptions are available for only a few. No new elements of design were introduced until toward the end of this period, and even then only as a hesitant prophecy of developments in the eighteenth century. Although 1700 has been chosen as the terminal date for this study, seventeenth-century principles appear to have governed the building of many meeting houses for another ten or twenty years, and on occasion to have been employed even later. During the late seventeenth century the main change in the larger towns was toward greater size and probably toward more skillful and elegant construction. In smaller communities more modest structures still appeared, such as the first meeting house at Derby, Conn., built 28 feet long, 20 feet wide, and 10 feet high in 1682 (*T.R.,* 121).

Regardless of dimensions, the later meeting houses generally had the entrance on the south side and the pulpit opposite. An exception was the rearranging of the Wallingford, Conn., meeting house (1678), where in 1691 the pulpit was moved to the west end (*T.R.,* 100). Abandoning the fixed altar of Anglican worship had made it possible to use the space across the east end for seating with pews or galleries. Additional seating continued to be provided by one or more galleries, which were evidently part of the original plan of twenty-five meeting houses and added later in twenty-one others. Lean-tos, which caused the cross-section more nearly to resemble a parish church, were included at Hadley, Mass., 1663 (*T.R.,* 22), and Hempstead, L.I., 1678 (*T.R.,* 316). A lean-to was added at Norwich, Conn., in 1689 (*T.R.,* 109) and considered at Branford, Conn., in 1699 (*T.R.*, II, 123). Porches with stairs appeared on the meeting houses of Newbury, Mass., 1661;[2] the Third Church of Boston, Mass., 1669;[3] and Stratford, Conn., 1680 (*T.R.*, 142). These stair porches undoubtedly played a part in the development of the tower and spire units of the eighteenth-century meeting houses, but a detailed history of these buildings is not yet available.

Additional gables or dormers were built on the roofs of eight meeting houses, and bell or watch turrets on twenty. The hip roof with crowning turret and balustrade, with or without dormers, seems to have been prominent among the larger meeting houses.

At the same time some medieval decorative elements were still in use, particularly the "pyramid," while the reference to "pendants" at Salem, Mass., for the second meeting house in 1670 may indicate some type of hammerbeam roof:

> . . . to putt under each Girth three Suitable pillers y[e] Middle Piller of the Three to be placed under y[e] East and West pendant & to be Substantiall & strong & to Sett up one Large piller under the Middle pendant of the Meeteing house. (*T.R.*, II, 201)

Another medieval survival was the separate frame for the bell, already mentioned at Dorchester, Mass., in 1678, continuing the tradition of separate bell-cotes in England.[4]

Contemporary drawings show the schemes of a few meeting houses, though the proportions are not represented accurately. The earliest so illustrated are the first building of the Third Church in Boston, Mass., and the second meeting house in New Haven, Conn., both built in 1669.

When the first meeting house of the Third Church in Boston was demolished in 1729, the *New England Weekly Journal* said that it was "near 75 foot long and near 51 wide; beside the Southern, Eastern and Western porches."[5] At the same time the *Boston Weekly News-Letter* reported:

> On Friday the 28th of Feb. last was kept as a Day of Fasting & Prayer by the South Church & Congregation in this Town, upon

occasion of taking down their Old Meeting-House, & Building a New One of Brick, which is to stand in the same Place. The last Lord's Day the Second of this Instant, was the last time of Meeting in their Old House, which has stood for Three-score Years the last January, since twas raised. On the Monday, the Workmen took down the Windows, the Pews, the Pulpit and the Seats both below and in the Galleries. On the Tuesday in the Forenoon, they took down the Belfry, the Porches, the Stairs and the Galleries themselves. In the Afternoon they drew off the Boards at both Ends and laid it open: and about Five a Clock, They turned over the whole remaining Part of the Building at one Draught into the Yard on the North side; in doing which, it fell all to pieces. Yesterday they employ'd in removing the Fragments. And when we came to examin the main Timbers, it was surprizing to see that the Bottoms of the Great Rafters which upheld the Roof, together with the hinder Beams which bore up the Galleries were quite decay'd with Rotteness: and the Ends of all the Summers, for Six or Eight foot were in a great measure turn'd to Powder; that nothing but the King posts and the other Frame above has for a long time kept them from tumbling down upon the People.[6]

According to the available records, this was the largest meeting house erected in New England during the seventeenth century. It appears as Number 10 on the Burgis "View of Boston," published in 1722. (FIGURE 18.) It is shown here with three gables on the long side and an enormous turret in the center. The turret is shown as an open structure on four posts, with a "pyramid" on each corner and a weathervane on top.

A déed of June 27, 1687, speaks of the Third Church meeting house as a "large spacious and faire meeting house with three large Porches every way compleatly fitted and covered with sheete lead, the house and said Porches." This is the earliest recorded use of lead as a covering for a meeting house roof in New England, and it was costly, for the deed goes on to say that it "stood them and their Associates neere if not above two thousand pounds more."[7]

Another type of roof familiar in the seventeenth century was built at New Haven in 1669. A map drawn by James Wadsworth in 1748 shows the meeting house on the Green, a two-story build-

FIGURE 18. Boston, Mass. Third Church. Meeting House I. 1669. William Burgis, "View of Boston," Number 10. 1722. *Courtesy Phelps Stokes Collection, The New York Public Library.*

ing with three doors on the front, five bays of windows in the second story, and a hip roof with dormers, turret, and weathervane. (FIGURE 19.)

In 1762 Ezra Stiles noted an addition of 25 feet, bringing the dimensions to about 60 feet by 55 feet.[8] A plan sketched in Stiles' *Itineraries* (FIGURE 20), with proportions not quite correct, shows the original building with the pulpit on the wall opposite the three front doors, posts for the gallery, and stairs to the gallery in each corner of the front. The two flanking doors on the front were indicated right in the corner, under the stairs, by both Wadsworth and Stiles. A body of seats was divided down the center, with women on the east and men on the west, long and short seats arranged around the walls, and then the addition back of the pulpit, again with seats and stairs to the gallery on the north wall. The roof was probably extended over the new portion in much the same way as the new roof at Hingham, Mass., in 1755. (Figure 24, below.) The Wadsworth map shows only a turret, with no platform or balustrade.

A third kind of roof is illustrated by a little drawing owned by the Pilgrim Society at Plymouth, Mass. (FIGURE 21.) The drawing, labeled "Meeting House Plymouth Built 1683," has been attributed to Samuel Davis (1765–1829).[9] If this is correct, Davis could not have seen the meeting house, which was demolished in 1744. Whether he made the drawing or not, the long gabled building shown does not indicate properly a building 45 feet long and 40 feet wide.

Between the inscription and the principal drawing there is, however, a smaller and much cruder drawing of a building, showing a cross-gabled roof with turret. It is important to note that at Weymouth, Mass., on December 18, 1682, it was voted to build a meeting house "45 feet in bredth and twenty foot stud between joints . . . ther shall be fower Gable ends of convenient hight to make it uniform . . . that Jacob Nash should be the man to build and finish" (*T.R.*, 162). The Weymouth meeting house was replaced in 1751 and could not have been seen by Davis either. The two buildings were about thirty miles apart, comparable in size, and the one at Plymouth had been voted only three months ear-

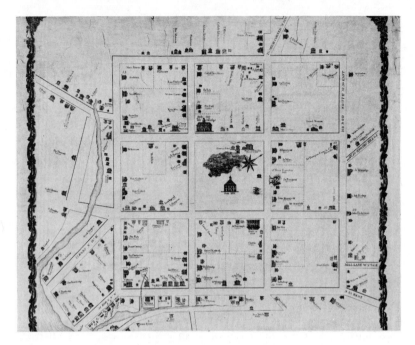

FIGURE 19. New Haven, Conn. Meeting House II. 1660. Wadsworth
Map. 1748. *Courtesy Yale University Map Collection.*

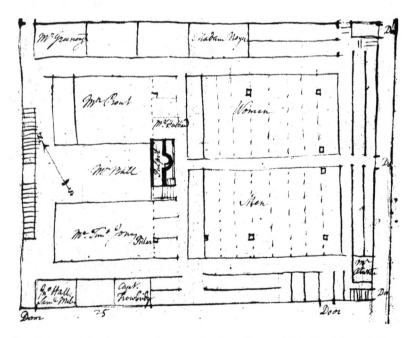

FIGURE 20. New Haven, Conn. Meeting House II. 1669. Plan. Stiles,
Itineraries, II, p. 414. *Courtesy Yale University Library.*

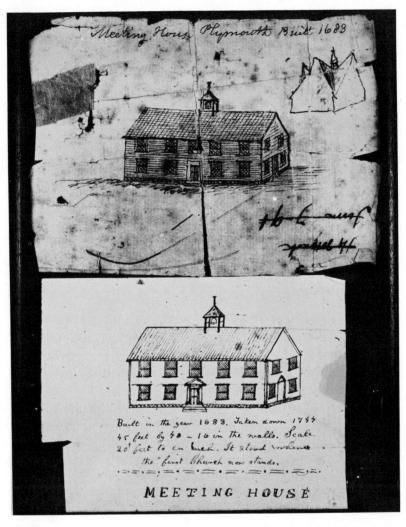

Built in the year 1683. Taken down 1744
45 feet by 40 - 16 in the walls. Scale
20' feet to an inch. It stood where
the first Church now stands.

MEETING HOUSE

FIGURE 21. Plymouth, Mass. Meeting House II. 1683. Sketches. *Courtesy Pilgrim Society, Plymouth.*

lier (*T.R.*, I, 171). The little sketch on the Plymouth drawing might be a correction by a person better informed than the original author. Certainly the Weymouth record indicates that this kind of roof was being built near-by at this time.

Small gables or dormers appear to have been included on the hip roof of the third meeting house at Deerfield, Mass., 1694. (FIGURE 22.) The model chosen was the first meeting house at Hatfield, Mass., 1668, to which east and west dormers had been added in 1689 (*T.R.*, II, 13). Two of the three Woodbridge sketches show such dormers. That these could be removed as well as added is attested by a vote at Newbury, Mass., in the winter of 1725/26

> that the four Gable end In ye Roof of ye meeting House be Taken Down and that each Part opened thereby be well Timbered and Boarded and Shingled up and made tite & Sound up to ye Platform in ye same form on Each side as hip Rafters now stand.[10]

It is not always possible to be certain which kind of roof was used on a meeting house, since references to "gables" can mean either full cross-gabled roofs or dormers. In the case of the third meeting house at Sudbury, Mass., 1687, the gables over which the town argued may have been dormers.[11]

The second meeting house at Hingham, Mass., 1681, is the only surviving example of a seventeenth-century meeting house in New England. In 1680 the inhabitants "agreed to build their new meeting house fifty five footes in length, and forty five in breadth, and twenty, or one and twenty footes to be the height of the posts, with galleries on one side and at both the ends" (*T.R.*, I, August 11, 1680). Stairs to the turret were ordered in March 1696, and the turret platform was mended in October (*T.R.*, I, March 30, October 23, 1696). Additional seats were built in 1702 and 1706, and in 1707 it was voted "to take down the glass that is in the East window of the meeting house over the pulpett and cause it to be cloased up" (*T.R.*, II, March 30, 1702; March 25, 1706; March 18, 1707/08). An addition of 14 feet on the northeast side was voted in 1728, the pulpit was moved to the new back wall in 1729, and the meeting house was ceiled in 1731.[12] A simi-

FIGURE 22. Deerfield, Mass. Meeting House III. 1694. Sketches. Wood-bridge, *Diary*, f.p. 337. *Courtesy Massachusetts Historical Society.*

lar addition on the southwest side was made in 1755, a new belfry and porches were built, and the present pulpit was placed on the northwest side.

By this time the building had been extensively altered and had taken on the appearance that it has today. The meeting house was restored in 1930, when the ceiling was removed and the nineteenth-century furnishings were replaced by eighteenth-century-type furnishings. Sections drawn at the time of restoration show the original frame. (FIGURES 23 AND 24.) Above the main body of the building, which has curved braces at the corners, the roof of the original portion is constructed with a system of king posts and curved trusses. The resemblance to an inverted ship's hull has earned the meeting house the nickname "Old Ship."

In its present form the building has often been cited as a typical example, as well as the only remaining one, of a seventeenth-century New England meeting house.[13] As it stands now, 73 feet long and 55 feet wide, it is larger than any of its contemporaries were, according to present knowledge, with the exception of the Third Church meeting house in Boston, Mass., 1669. The size is therefore misleading, as is the shape of the enlarged roof, the present placement of doors and windows, and the eighteenth-century belfry.

The conjectural drawing of the front elevation (FIGURE 25) is an attempt to visualize more correctly what the meeting house looked like in 1682. The original southwest front of the building is shown with a hip roof, platform, and turret, gables on each side, two doors, two windows in each story, and a small window in the gable. Traces of the dormers were found in the restoration of 1930.[14] The small window in the gable is drawn the size of a window preserved in the Hingham meeting house, which consists of two casements each 19½ inches by 21½ inches.[15] The drawing cannot be more than an approximation of the original appearance of the building, which merits a careful modern study of the remaining original structure.

As for the interior, the galleries are under the additions on the sides, with the pulpit on the northwest side. The galleries

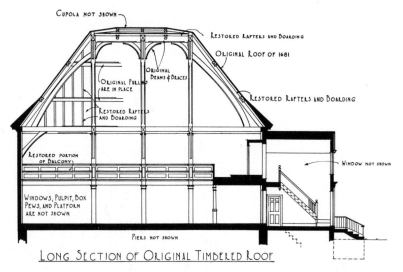

FIGURE 23. Hingham, Mass. Meeting House II. 1681. Longitudinal section. Corse, "The Old Ship Meeting House," p. 24. *Courtesy* Old Time New England.

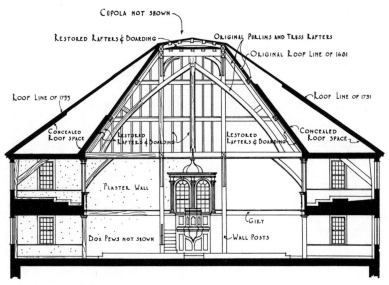

FIGURE 24. Hingham, Mass. Meeting House II. 1681. Cross section. Corse, "The Old Ship Meeting House," p. 25. *Courtesy* Old Time New England.

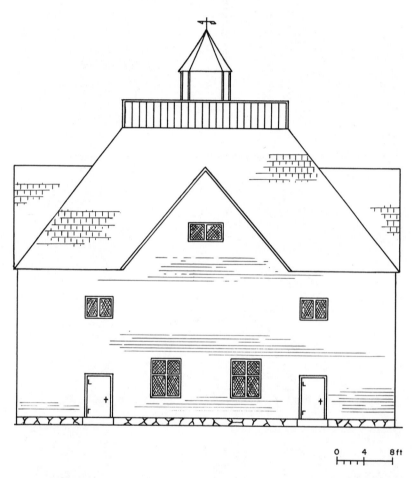

FIGURE 25. Hingham, Mass. Meeting House II. 1681. *Conjectural elevation: Author.*

were on three sides in the original building, with the pulpit on the northeast side, and the meeting house was more crowded than it is now. The galleries may have left only a small well for the pulpit. When the gallery was built on the southwest end of the meeting house at Marblehead, Mass., in 1663, it was to be built "from the pricke posts and soe to the end of the House" (*T.R.*, 229). Again, on March 18, 1668/69, the northeast gallery was ordered at Marblehead "from the prickt post and soe to the end of the House" (*T.R.*, 248). In the diagram for a dormer roof published by Michael Hoare in 1728, the "prick posts" are intermediate posts set along the beam between the king post and plate.[16] Such posts are shown in the framing diagram of the Hingham meeting house, following the lines of the platform (Figure 24). With the description of the galleries at Marblehead, the definition of a "prick post" by Hoare and the existence of such posts in the framing at Hingham, it is possible but not necessary that the galleries at Hingham followed the line of these posts and consequently occupied a large portion of the meeting house. (FIGURE 26.)

When the effects of addition and restoration on the Hingham meeting house are taken into consideration, it appears that the building is not an adequate guide to the lost meeting houses of the seventeenth century. Records of the destroyed buildings, enlightened by study of contemporary builders' guides and knowledge of carpentry techniques in domestic architecture of the same period, provide more valuable information than this still extant but substantially altered example.

Another type of meeting house has already been noted at Enfield, Conn., in 1684, where there was a vote for a "house for the ministry if any come to be built as also a meeting house" (*T.R.*, I, 77). The combination of minister's dwelling and meeting house is rare at the end of the century.

In spite of the proximity of the Dutch to the towns of southern Connecticut, very little Dutch influence on meeting houses has been detected. A notable exception appears to have occurred very late in the century at Fairfield, Conn. The third meeting house at Fairfield, 1698, was described by the English traveler

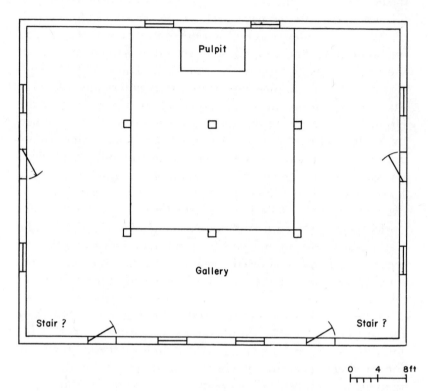

FIGURE 26. Hingham, Mass. Meeting House II. 1681. *Conjectural plan: Author.*

Alexander Hamilton in 1744 as follows: "Fairfield, which is another town in which is an octogonall church or meeting built of wood like that of Jamaica upon Long Island, upon the cupolo of which is a public clock."[17]

The Dutch Reformed Church in Jamaica, built in 1715, was evidently hexagonal rather than octagonal, and was a late example of the kind of church erected by the Dutch settlers.[18] No other octagonal or hexagonal Congregational meeting house is at present known to have been built in New England during the seventeenth century. The English settlers do not seem to have been anxious to imitate the Dutch churches, even though the latter were built for an equally vigorous Protestant worship.

The change from Congregational meeting house to Congregational church in New England came about slowly and was not fully accomplished until the beginning of the nineteenth century. The earliest known church with tower and spire at one end was the Brattle Street Church in Boston, Mass., 1699. By this time Wren and his contemporaries in England had brought the English Renaissance parish churches to their first full development. The Brattle Street Church may have been the earliest of the New England meeting houses to follow English fashion, at least on the exterior.

The Burgis "View" (FIGURE 27) shows a two-story building with a gable roof with balustrade, and with a square tower at one end, which has belfry windows, another balustrade, spire, and weathervane. From the *Itineraries* of Ezra Stiles comes the information that the building was 72 feet long and 52 feet wide, the largest known since the Third Church meeting house in Boston, Mass., 1669.[19]

The first meeting in the Brattle Street Church was held on December 24, 1699, the sermon being preached from II *Chronicles* 6:18: "But will God in very deed dwell with men on the earth? behold, heaven and the heaven of heavens cannot contain thee; how much less this house which I have built!" It is interesting to find this choice of text, suggesting the sanctity of the building, which the Puritans had denied, coinciding with the first

FIGURE 27. Boston, Mass. Brattle Street Church I. 1699. Burgis, "View of Boston," Number 27. 1722. *Courtesy Phelps Stokes Collection, The New York Public Library.*

presently known use of end tower and spire and also the first documentary mention of the building as a "church."[20]

In the same period, between the Restoration of 1660 and the Toleration Act of 1689, the fortunes of Nonconformists in England varied. The new Parliament of Charles II met on May 8, 1661, and the bishops returned to the House of Lords on November 30. Soon after, on January 10, a proclamation was issued "for restraining all seditious meetings and conventicles under pretence of religious worship, and forbidding any meetings for worship, except in parochial churches or chapels, or in private houses by the residents."[21] This still left hundreds of parish livings to Congregational or Presbyterian ministers who had held them during the Interregnum. A more severe measure was taken against these men in the Act for the Uniformity of Public Prayers (May 19, 1662), which re-established the use of the Prayer Book and the necessity of episcopal ordination.[22] Those who refused to conform by St. Bartholomew's Day, August 24, were ejected from their churches and replaced by Anglican clergy.

By the same act French and Dutch Protestants were given protection for worship: "Provided, that the penalties in this act shall not extend to the foreigners or aliens of the foreign reformed churches, allowed or to be allowed by the king's majesty, his heirs and successors, in England."[23] These foreign congregations continued to use certain allowed places, such as the chapel of St. Julian in Southampton and the crypt at Canterbury, since they were still not building their own churches in England.[24]

Charles II tried to provide some toleration for Nonconformists and also for Roman Catholics by a proposed Declaration, (December 26, 1662):

> We do declare a liberty to tender consciences, and that so no man shall be disquieted or called in question for differences of opinion in matters of religion, which do not disturb the peace of the kingdom: and that we shall be ready to consent to such an act of parliament, as upon mature deliberation shall be offered to us for the full granting of that indulgence.[25]

81

But Parliament was not sympathetic to any dissenting sects, and more than a quarter of a century passed before the Nonconformists were granted any lasting freedom of worship.

The history of English Nonconformist architecture begins in this period. Although most dissenting congregations met for worship in private houses, some did build "chapels" or "meeting houses" in London and elsewhere. Two major obstacles were laid in the way of dissenting worship, the Conventicle Act and the Five Mile Act. The former, effective July 1, 1664, made it an offence for more than five persons to unite in religious worship except in the Church of England.[26] The latter, effective March 24, 1665, provided, among other things, "that all those who preached in conventicles or meetings, contrary to the statutes of the realm, shall not come within five miles of a corporation."[27] In spite of these restrictions, certain meeting places were provided by various congregations. Most of them came to the attention of the authorities, and it is largely in official complaints that they are recorded.

In private houses rooms seem to have been cleared and fitted with pulpits, sometimes also with seats or benches. A particularly interesting arrangement was made in the house bought by the Rev. Thomas Jolly, ejected from Altham Chapel in the parish of Whalley, Lancs.:

> In his house there was a stair case leading from the common sitting-room, and at the bottom of the staircase was a door so constructed that the upper half could be made to fall back on brackets and form a pulpit. As soon as an alarm was given outside the house, the upper part of the door was raised again and the preacher could escape upstairs.[28]

Some houses were adapted for large numbers of people by the use of movable partitions between rooms. Mr. Seth Wood's meeting house in Blackfriars, London, for instance, consisted of "four rooms opening into each other, with lattice partitions; each room being conveniently fitted up with benches and forms."[29] Similarly the meeting house of the Moravian Brethren in Fetter Lane "is said to have consisted of four rooms opening into each other, and contained seventeen pews and divers benches; also to have had two entrances, in order that the preacher, when danger was near, might be able to escape."[30] At Broadmead, Bristol, mention is made of "four great rooms made into one square room, about sixteen yards long, and fifteen yards broad."[31] Certainly not all private houses used as meeting houses were partitioned or even necessarily had pulpits, but the Nonconformist congregations appear to have arranged appropriate settings for their services whenever possible.

In some cases they were bold enough to build regular "meeting houses," as they came to be called in the 1660's. The Rev. Thomas Vincent's meeting house in Hand Alley, Bishopsgate, London, is described as "a large place with three galleries, thirty large pews, and many benches and forms."[32] It was built sometime after 1662, used for Anglican services after the Fire of London, and pulled down sometime after 1729. Another was the Independent meeting house in Miles Lane, described in 1672 as a "Howse or Roome."[33]

Several other meeting houses were built in London in the 1660's and also a few in other towns. The chapel in Monks Lane, Corsham, Wilts., may have been built as a "five-mile" chapel after the Five Mile Act of 1665.[34] (FIGURE 28.) Attempts to document the date of this building have so far been unsuccessful. It is presently arranged with galleries on three sides, pews and pulpit opposite. A Presbyterian meeting house is recorded in Pendennis, Cornwall, in 1668,[35] and one of the largest outside London was built at Yarmouth, Norfolk, in 1669.

Frequent documentary notices from 1667 onwards indicate the size and industry of the Yarmouth Independent congregation. After some years of meeting in private houses, it was reported on March 3, 1669, that "the Independents have fitted up a place for public meetings, with seats for the people, and a desk for the parson, where at least 1,000 meet." The account adds that the "fitting up was not taken notice of before they met, only by their own party."[36] This place may have been the house of Alderman Thomas Raven, on the island of Lovingland, where the Independents met, at least at intervals, between 1667 and 1670.[37]

FIGURE 28. Corsham, Wilts. Monks Lane Chapel. Late 17th Century? *Photo: Geoffrey N. Wright.*

Another report on March 22 remarked that, "the new meeting-place being found too little to contain the people that flock thither, they are erecting 3 fair galleries."[38] And on April 14 a further report said that "Their new meeting-place has become too little to receive them, and a member informed me that if this toleration continues, they shall erect a fair church in our south end."[39]

By June 1670 there were so many meeting houses that even Christopher Wren was called upon to get them pulled down. The order referred to places fitted for meetings "under pretence of religious worship." Wren was to "cause to be pulled down and secured in safe places, all pulpits, benches, and other seats, he shall find in any of the houses aforesaid for the convenience of the conventicles."[40] A particular instance was at Bermondsey, Surrey, where on July 22, 1670, Wren was ordered "to pull down the barn called the Jamaica Barn."[41]

Another solution for Nonconformist worship was found in the guildhalls. Several are known to have been so used in London in the late 1660's, such as Glovers Hall in Beach Lane.[42] Some town halls or moot halls in provincial towns had been used for services for a number of years, as at Bury St. Edmunds, Suffolk,[43] and Chard, Somerset,[44] although after the Restoration services like these became illegal.

Hoping to increase his popularity and gain support in the war against the Dutch, Charles II issued another Declaration of Indulgence on March 15, 1672:

And that there may be no pretence for any of our subjects to continue their illegal meetings and conventicles, we do declare, that we shall from time to time allow a sufficient number of places, as they shall be desired, in all parts of this our kingdom, for the use of such as do not conform to the church of England, to meet and assemble in in order to their public worship and devotion; which places shall be open and free to all persons. . . . our express will and pleasure is, that none of our subjects do presume to meet in any place, until such place be allowed, and the teacher of that congregation be approved by us.[45]

The ensuing rush for licenses, which amounted to about 2,500, was halted abruptly when the king, under pressure from Parliament, revoked the Declaration on March 3, 1673.[46] Licenses had been requested for many private houses, at least twenty-nine town halls, and eleven schoolhouses, as well as for the ministers who were to preach in them. Most of the places had probably already been in use for dissenting services prior to the Declaration.

On the strength of the Declaration several more meeting houses appear to have been built in 1672. Some of the license applications speak of a "new built meeting place," as at Delp, Derbys., or Winkle in Prestbury, Ches.[47] Very little is known about these buildings, and none has survived, as far as it has been possible to determine. The Yarmouth meeting house, 1673–74, was "50 foot one way and 60 the other, with a gallery quite round it close to the pulpit, with six seats in it, one behind the other, and all accommodation possible for the reception of people below."[48] These were the dimensions of the Salem, Mass., meeting house of 1670, and the gallery "close to the pulpit" recalls the arrangements already discussed for the meeting houses at Marblehead, Mass., 1663, and Hingham, Mass., 1681.

According to a later historian, the Mill Hill Chapel at Leeds, Yorks., was built "more Ecclesiastico," with a row of pillars and arches,[49] but the chapel was replaced in 1847 and no further description has been found.

Several Nonconformist meeting houses were built in London about 1672, some reportedly with galleries on three sides,[50] though no particularly detailed descriptions are available for any of these structures. Some congregations persisted in building even after the revocation of the Declaration of Indulgence. The most complete and interesting description of one of their meeting houses seems to be in the contract for the meeting house in Nightingale Lane (May 8, 1682).[51] This timber meeting house with tarred weatherboarding and tile roof must have been colorful, especially with the windows and doors in "oyle colouring," whatever that color may have been. It was rebuilt in 1722.

The long controversy between Nonconformist and Anglican

came to a partial settlement after the Revolution of 1688 with An Act for Exempting their Majesties Protestant Subjects, Dissenting from the Church of England, from the Penalties of Certain Laws, commonly known as the Toleration Act (May 24, 1689).[52] Among the provisions which made public Nonconformist worship possible, Number XIX applied to the places of worship:

> Provided always, that no congregation or assembly of religious worship shall be permitted or allowed by this act, until the place of such meeting be certified to the bishop of the diocese, or to the archdeacon of that archdeaconry, or to the justices of the peace at the general or quarter sessions of the peace for the county, city or place in which such meeting shall be held, and registered in the said bishop's or archdeacon's court respectively, or recorded at the said general or quarter sessions; the register, or clerk of the peace thereof respectively, is hereby required to register the same, and to give certificate thereof to such person as shall demand the same, for which there shall be no greater fee or reward taken, than the sum of sixpence.[53]

No specification is made as to the kind of building to be registered for worship, nor that the building was to be used for worship only. Briggs gives 2,418 buildings registered by Congregationalists, Baptists, and Presbyterians between 1689 and 1700, many of which were private houses.[54]

Of the extant meeting houses, sometimes called "chapels," built immediately after the Toleration Act, a few of particular interest may be noted. A rectangular building with a pulpit on one of the long sides and possibly galleries on the other three was the type generally adopted. In a small group of chapels in Cheshire the galleries were entered by outside stairs (forestairs) at either end, and the principal entrances were under these stairs.[55]

An example of a meeting house built in a row of houses and thus concealed among them may be found in the Baptist Chapel at Tewkesbury, Glos., built 1690. (FIGURE 29.) According to a notice posted in the chapel, "except that about a hundred years ago, the left and right gallery portions were parted off to form two cottages, the fabric remains untouched." If today the Tewkes-

FIGURE 29. Tewkesbury, Glos. Baptist Chapel. 1690. *Photo: Author.*

bury chapel is more enclosed by surrounding buildings than formerly, it at least illustrates how such a meeting house might have been hidden during the seventeenth century.

The meeting houses at Norwich, Norfolk, 1693, and Ipswich, Suffolk, 1700, are among the largest and most elaborate of this group and show Nonconformist architecture in seventeenth-century England now fully developed.[56] Both are two-story buildings with galleries on three sides and the pulpit at the middle of the fourth side. The Old Meeting at Norwich is brick with hipped roof and modillioned cornice, divided into five bays on the front by a giant Corinthian order. (FIGURE 30.) The galleries are carried on Tuscan columns and the ceiling beams on Doric columns with entablature blocks. According to an unsigned and undated pamphlet history, "the present arrangement of the pews in curving banks was made at the end of the last century from the oak of the original ones."

The Friars Street Chapel in Ipswich was begun by the carpenter Joseph Clark in 1699 and finished in 1700. (FIGURE 31.) It is 60 feet long and 50 feet wide, with two parallel roofs supported on columns on the long axis of the building, as in the rebuilt chapel at Walpole, Suffolk, and later at Wattisfield, Suffolk, and Bury St. Edmunds, Suffolk.[57] Like Old Meeting at Norwich, the Ipswich chapel is notable for generous detail. Richly pedimented doorways with elliptical windows above on the front and four round-headed windows with circular windows above on the pulpit wall opposite contribute to an imposing effect. This is repeated on the interior with fine panelling on the box pews and galleries and an elaborate hexagonal pulpit. The contract for the chapel, which is timber-framed, is preserved.[58]

With such meeting houses Nonconformist building in England entered quickly into its first mature period, many years after meeting house architecture was firmly established in New England. It remains now to inquire where the New England meeting houses may be most reasonably placed in the history of post-Reformation architecture.

FIGURE 30. Norwich, Norfolk. Old Meeting. 1693. *Photo: Author.*

FIGURE 31. Ipswich, Suffolk. Friars Street Chapel. 1700. *Photo: Author.*

CHAPTER SIX

The New England Meeting House as Puritan Architecture

W HEN THE presently available information is examined, it becomes clear that by 1642 the basic requirements for a house of worship in Puritan New England had been determined. A room with a pulpit toward the center of one wall and a table were all that were actually necessary for Congregational services during the seventeenth century.

According to the size and prosperity of a town, its meeting house might in addition have one or more galleries, built-in pews, a belfry, and some architectural ornament. Sizes and shapes of the buildings varied, as did the types of roof, which included gabled, cross-gabled, and hip roofs, with or without dormers, platforms, and turrets.

The extent of possible variations, exterior and interior, indicates that no single kind of building for a meeting house was in the minds of the colonists either before their departure from England or immediately upon their arrival in Massachusetts Bay. All of the possible major elements of a meeting house were included in a number of large and mature designs in the last quarter of the century, but these designs were not fully developed in the 1630's, nor were they always used fifty years later. Had there been an English or Continental model which doctrinal considerations compelled the Puritans to follow, this would have been evident in a more consistent building program.

91

Yet very soon after the beginning of the Great Migration the colonists did start to build structures for public worship and assembly, the idea of a building to combine both functions apparently having occurred to them quite promptly.

As for public worship, there can be little doubt that the location of the pulpit in New England followed that in the English parish church after the Reformation. No comparable location for the pulpit, against one long wall, has come to light among the Continental Protestant churches before 1630. The closest are the Dutch pulpits, placed against centrally located piers in the conversion of medieval buildings. The Puritans were not so hostile to all that they had known in England that they built their meeting houses in deliberate defiance of English tradition. Had this been the case, the New England pulpits would have been placed differently, perhaps on a parquet in the midst of the congregation, as in some Huguenot temples, or at the end of the long axis, as in some of the Lutheran churches.

The quarrel between Puritan and Anglican was not so much over the pulpit as over the communion table, and here practices differed sharply. The Puritan distribution of the bread and wine of the Lord's Supper to communicants seated in their pews emphasized the communal rather than the sacrificial aspect of the rite. If the communion table in New England had an early definite location, this is not evident from the documents, although later records show that it came to be placed in front of the pulpit. Fixed pews were eventually built across the east end of the building in the space occupied by the altar or communion table in England.

In this respect the New England meeting houses differ from the seventeenth-century churches of the South, which were Church of England. In these buildings the pulpit might be on one side, but the altar was set behind a rail at the east end. This was the original plan of Merchant's Hope Church in Prince George County, Va., 1657.[1] (FIGURE 32.) The same arrangement was probably also used in the later Wye Church, near Wye Mills, Talbot County, Md., 1717.[2] These and other Southern churches were built for Anglican worship, and there is no reason to believe

FIGURE 32. Prince George County, Va. Merchant's Hope Church. 1657. *Photo: Author.*

FIGURE 33. Melverly, Salop. St. Peter's Church. 1588. *Photo: Courtesy National Monuments Record.*

that the location of their pulpits was influenced by Puritan theology.

The Anglican churches in the colonial South, therefore, used the interior arrangement already familiar in England, as described in Chapter III. The New England builders retained part of this arrangement, the location of the pulpit, and to this extent at least the English parish church was one of the sources for meeting house design.

As for the exterior of the meeting houses, even in the first period a variety may be demonstrated. Both the small meeting house at Dedham, Mass., 1638, and the larger one at Hampton, N.H., 1640, were rectangular with gable roofs. A belfry was present from the first at Hampton and was added later at Dedham. Without a belfry such a building would resemble a dwelling. With a belfry the Hampton meeting house probably looked much like Melverley, St. Peter's Church, Salop., 1588, where the dimensions are comparable (44 feet by 22 feet; Hampton, 40 feet by 22 feet).[3] (FIGURE 33.)

At the same time the meeting houses had certain important features in common with another group of English buildings: the town halls or market halls. (For convenience, the term *market hall* is intended to cover all such buildings, including town halls, moot halls, and guild halls.)

Most of the late sixteenth- and early seventeenth-century market halls of England have disappeared, but enough remain, along with a few prints of former buildings, to make some comparison possible. For one matter, while the English parish churches were generally placed beside the road, the market halls were usually placed out in the town square, market place, or in the middle of the High Street. The same was often true of the New England meeting houses, as at Easthampton, L.I., 1652 (*T.R.*, II, map f. p. 12); Hadley, Mass., 1663 (*T.R.*, 22), and Middletown, Conn., 1670 (*T.R.*, 97), as well as in the more classical planning of the Green in New Haven, Conn., in 1638.[4] In Concord, Mass., and some of the other towns, the meeting house served as the official center of the town lands.

For the second half of the century enough records remain to

show clearly the repetition of market hall types in the colonies. A plain rectangular building with a gable roof had been chosen for numerous market halls, such as those at Elstow, Beds., begun in the fifteenth century, and Ledbury, Herts., about 1633. (FIGURES 34 AND 35.) These buildings are not distinguishable from houses or chapels as a type except in being raised on posts, as was customary, with the market stalls beneath. Occasionally a hip roof was used, as at Dullingham, Cambs., or a double roof, as at Thaxted, Essex. (FIGURES 36 AND 37.)

More specifically a market house type is the cross-gabled building with turret, such as the one at Market Harborough, Leics., 1618. (FIGURE 38.) Just how early this type was used for New England meeting houses is uncertain. A group built in the 1680's and 1690's indicates some popularity of this construction late in the century. According to tradition, though not fully documented, the meeting house at Beverly, Mass., 1682, had a cross-gabled roof. It was so illustrated in 1843, although it had been replaced in 1770.[5] Possibly also cross-gabled was the one at Sudbury, Mass., 1687, as well as those at Weymouth, Mass., 1682, and Plymouth, Mass., 1683, which have already been discussed.

The meeting houses with hip roofs and turrets pose a different problem whether square or rectangular. The earliest square meeting house known, or suspected, was the one built in Cambridge, Mass., about 1632. No turret is recorded here, and the building may have resembled the Court House at New Buckenham, Norfolk, with its hip roof and pinnacle. (FIGURE 39.) The earliest square meeting house known to have had a turret and balustraded platform was at New Haven, Conn., 1640 (*T.R.*, 145), which had at least a turret if not a platform.

The rectangular type with hip roof, platform, and turret does not appear in the records until 1667, when it almost certainly was used at York, Me.[6] Originally the Hingham, Mass., meeting house of 1681 was built in this manner, though the additions have obscured the former proportions.

Early in the seventeenth century the square or rectangular building with hip roof, balustraded platform, and turret was well established in the domestic and civic architecture of Flanders

FIGURE 34. Elstow, Beds. Moot Hall. 15th Century. *Photo: Author.*

FIGURE 35. Ledbury, Herts. Market Hall. c. 1633. *Photo: Author.*

FIGURE 36. Dullingham, Cambs. Guildhall. 15th Century? *Photo: Author.*

FIGURE 37. Thaxted, Essex. Guildhall. 15th Century. *Photo: Author.*

FIGURE 38. Market Harborough, Leics. Market Hall. 1618. *Photo: Author*.

FIGURE 39. New Buckenham, Norfolk. Court House. 15th Century? *Photo: Author. Reprinted courtesy* Journal of the Society of Architectural Historians.

and Holland.[7] From the Low Countries this type of building quickly made its way to England. Several great houses were built in this manner, notably Coleshill, Berks., 1650, and also Wisbech Castle, Cambs., 1658; Thorney Abbey, Cambs., 1660; Horseheath, Cambs., 1663; and Kingston Lacy, Dorset, 1663–65.[8] Even before these, the principle was apparently well enough known to have been applied in one of the colonies in 1639, though not in New England. The Governor's Castle at St. Mary's City, Md., is believed to have been 54 feet square with a hip roof, balustraded platform, and cupola.[9]

It is unlikely, however, that the meeting houses of this type were derived from private houses when the type was also in use for public buildings, in England as well as in Holland. Among the most elaborate still extant in England are such market halls as those at Abingdon, Berks., 1678; Amersham, Bucks., 1682; and King's Lynn, Norfolk, 1683, all done after the Restoration and representing fashion and prosperity in the towns. Although raised above the market stalls, the main blocks of these buildings differ from the York and Hingham type of meeting house only in the use of brick rather than timber and in the application of classical detail. Another market hall which has been overlooked in this connection is the first Town House in Boston, Mass., 1657–58. This was 66 feet by 36 feet, set upon posts, and has cross-dormers, a balustraded platform, and two turrets.[10] Comparison with the more famous meeting house at Hingham shows that the later building was a survival of a well-established type.

Some of the shapes and schemes of New England meeting houses can thus be shown to be more like those of the English market halls than of any ecclesiastical model of the early seventeenth century.[11] The colonists' free use of a variety of possibilities in domestic architecture has previously been observed.

The resemblances, then, between the various kinds of town halls and the various kinds of meeting houses are not surprising in view of the uses of meeting houses in New England and the uses of the churches and market halls of England. Long before the identity between church membership and civil authority and franchise was established in New England, parish and town af-

54016

fairs in England had been interdependent. The parish church had no effective rival until after the Restoration, when the Nonconformists organized their own congregations in greater numbers. It was the vestry which saw to local taxes and the maintenance of highways and other civic needs, thereby setting a precedent in everyday business that made this aspect of the "theocratic commonwealth" quite natural to establish in New England.

Among many references to use of the church for purposes other than worship is found the question addressed by Bishop Brian Duppa to the churchwardens of Sussex in 1638: "Have there been kept in the church, chapel or churchyard, any plays, feasts, suppers, church ales, temporal courts, or Last Day juries, musters or meetings for rates and taxations, especially at the Communion table?"[12]

In like manner, the market place in England had served religious purposes, particularly the custom of preaching at the market cross and the "lectures" in the market halls in the sixteenth century. The market hall itself had as its forerunner the village cross, at the foot of which the market folk displayed their wares. To enlarge the single standing cross to an arcade and provide the sellers with a canopy, as so splendidly done at Malmesbury, Wilts., for example, was a reasonable development. The next step was to put a room above in which the courts could meet, and the town hall was complete. The term *market cross* is still occasionally applied to the complete building.

The lines of distinction in use between the church and the market hall were blurred enough in England that when the colonists put up buildings for two kinds of public assembly, they could find the market hall as likely a model as the church. Francis Johnson, in rejecting a consecrated place of worship, had said:

> . . . now there is not any one place holy, and peculiarly consecrate to the ministration of the Lords supper, as there was of old for sacrifice onely at Jerusalem.
>
> So as now therefore a place being a generall circumstance that perteyneth to all actions, commodius and necessarie for people to meet in together, and to be kept from injurie and unseasonableness of the weather.[13]

The same viewpoint was expressed by Richard Mather, writing about 1648: "There is no just ground from scripture to apply such a trope as church to a house for public assembly."[14]

Specific mention of a connection between meeting house and market is found so far only for Charlestown, Mass., where on February 5, 1651/52, "the generall Towne Agreed and determined to grant no more shops to be sett up by any on any syde of the meeting hous" (*T.R.*, February 5, 1651/52). Here is another instance of the meeting house being the site of the market.

The meeting houses appear to have differed from the English market halls in one important respect, that of the posts on which the latter were normally raised. For only one of the New England buildings are posts suggested, at Norwalk, Conn., in 1656 (*T.R.*, 29). This was one of the smaller meeting houses, 30 feet long and 18 feet wide. In view of the sparseness of the early records and the relatively late mention of these posts, the possibility must be left open that there were other meeting houses so built.

In materials and methods of construction, English village traditions were transferred to New England and have been well studied in domestic architecture. The few remaining houses are fortunately supplemented by documentary accounts. The material remains of public buildings are almost nonexistent, and the documents are scattered and incomplete, in spite of the wealth of information in them. Lack of visual evidence has discouraged some students of the meeting houses from thinking of them as medieval buildings. Yet the instructions in town records for framing, daubing, thatching, etc., do not belong to the new era of the English Renaissance but to the survival of late medieval practices, as is known for domestic buildings, such as the Turner House at Salem, Mass., 1668, and the Parson Capen House at Topsfield, Mass., 1683.

The meeting house at Dorchester, Mass., was the scene of a small accident on March 19, 1632:

> Mr. Maverick, one of the ministers of Dorchester, in drying a little powder, (which took fire by the heat of the fire pan,) fired a small barrel of two or three pounds, yet did no other harm but

singed his clothes. It was in the new meeting-house, which was thatched, and the thatch only blacked a little.[15]

This building could not have differed greatly from the church at Melverley, nor from the church built in the fort at Jamestown, Va., in 1610.[16] (FIGURE 40.) As the records throughout the seventeenth century are studied, it becomes apparent that the distinctive external features which appear in the meeting houses are those found in contemporary English village architecture.

Joshua Scottow, writing in 1694, was one of the first to deprecate the early "Mud-wall Meeting house" and to assert that "Our Ancestors were men of God . . . they Served God in Houses of the first Edition, without large Chambers, or Windows, Cieled with Cedar, or painted with Vermilion."[17] Historians, particularly in the nineteenth century, have made much of Puritanical fortitude in rude buildings.

But contemporary observers, who looked on the first meeting houses as part of a normal and familiar building program in the towns, expressed more generous opinions. David Pieterez de Vries, a Dutch voyager, spoke of the Hartford, Conn., meeting house of 1635 as "a fine church."[18] Thomas Lechford, who gave such an explicit description of New England worship in 1642, added: "The publique worship is in as faire a meeting house as they can provide, wherein, in most places, they have been at great charges."[19]

Edward Johnson's *A History of New-England* (1654) described the Charlestown, Mass., meeting house of 1640 as "very comly built and large" and the one of Ipswich, Mass., in 1646 as "beautifully built," both in contrast to his comment on the Roxbury, Mass., meeting house of 1632 as "destitute and unbeautified with other buildings."[20] Samuel Maverick also spoke appreciatively of the "two handsome Churches" in Boston and the "very stately Church" in New Haven, Conn., in 1660. Maverick's further remark that "there are many good farmes belonging to Bostone, which have a Metting House, as it were a Chapel of Ease," suggests some application of this practice of parish organization in New England.[21]

FIGURE 40. Jamestown, Va. Fort Church. Reconstruction as of 1610. *Photo: Author.*

FIGURE 41. Winslow, Bucks. Baptist Chapel. 1695. *Photo: Author.*

In addition to inquiry about the sources of the meeting houses some attention may be given to their consequences beyond the continuation and transformation of their characteristics in the eighteenth century. Although many valuable studies have been made of individual meeting houses built between 1700 and 1789 and still standing, no authoritative history of the whole period has appeared in which the records of lost buildings are added to the available evidence. The most dramatic impact of the mid-seventeenth-century meeting houses was on the Nonconformist chapels of England built during the last decade of the century, after the Toleration Act. Here, in such chapels as those of Norwich and Ipswich (Figures 30 and 31), the internal arrangements were clearly derived from New England, with the pulpit on one long side, and pews and galleries facing it on the other three sides. If the earliest New England meeting houses owed the concept of placing the pulpit on one long side of the building to Post-Reformation parish church planning in England, the later meeting houses returned to England a further logically developed plan for dissenting worship.

The English Congregational and Presbyterian chapels are built of brick or stone rather than wood, and the more elaborate ones are carried out in the mode of the day with little hesitation about ornament. The giant Corinthian order and generous cornice on the Old Meeting at Norwich give a wall treatment nearly as rich as that of the King's Lynn Custom House nearby, built in 1683.[22]

Much simpler is the Baptist Chapel at Winslow, Bucks., 1695, built of brick, 24 feet long and 16½ feet wide, with virtually no detail.[23] (FIGURE 41.) The dimensions of the Winslow chapel are slightly smaller than those of the meeting house at Northampton, Mass., 1655, which was 26 feet long and 18 feet wide.[24] The larger chapel at Winterburn, Yorks., 41 feet long and 24½ feet wide, is built of stone with quoins at the corners, and is in two stories of five bays on the front (south) side, with the door in the middle bay. (FIGURE 42.) The chapel looks like the side-entrance meeting houses still remaining from the eighteenth century in New England and if built in timber would bear a striking resemblance

FIGURE 42. Winterburn, Yorks. Chapel. Late 17th Century. *Photo: Author.*

FIGURE 43. Sandown, N.H. Meeting House. 1773. *Photo: Author.*

to one such as the Sandown, N.H., meeting house of 1773. (FIGURE 43.)

Unfortunately, not enough is known from the end of the seventeenth century nor have the documents of the early eighteenth century been searched sufficiently to make clear the time at which the gable roof became the dominant form on the larger New England meeting houses. There is also the possibility that the accident of the survival of the Hingham meeting house has brought undue emphasis on the use of the hip roof and that the rectangular meeting house with gable roof had been more familiar throughout the seventeenth century than has often been credited.

Regardless of these problems, however, some of the Nonconformist chapels of England show a definite reliance of New England models. Some attention has been given to the role that English market halls probably played in the development of the meeting houses, and in this connection a curious inversion has been found concerning the English chapels. In at least two instances Nikolaus Pevsner has noted a relation between chapel and market hall. Of the Town Hall at Hadleigh, Suffolk, 1851, he says that it is "red brick, round-arched like a Nonconformist Chapel, i.e., with a five-bay front, and windows higher up between."[25] Then again at Great Bardfield, Essex, he finds the Town Hall, 1859, "looking exactly like a Nonconformist chapel."[26] The history of the seventeenth-century relation between the two types of buildings suggests that the comparison should more properly have been put the other way around.

It is not the major purpose of this investigation to determine whether the New England meeting houses were representative of a Protestant or Puritan "aesthetic." Protestant they were in their lack of the furnishings and accessories necessary for Roman Catholic worship, as was also true of Anglican churches. They may be further distinguished as Puritan rather than Anglican by the arrangement of seats to face the pulpit rather than the communion table. Beyond this, efforts to find a sectarian identity in the meeting houses are less convincing.

The Massachusetts Bay colonists made no radical break with

English building tradition in the first years of settlement. When neither brick nor stone was available at reasonable cost, as was brick in Virginia, houses, meeting houses, and other buildings were timber-framed according to well-known structural methods. As the long history of timber churches in England shows, the use of wood did not in itself make any building "Puritan."

The formal elements of the meeting houses, dimensions, roofing, covering, materials, extent of panelling and turned work, porches, turrets, etc., were used with such variety that the term "Puritan" does not adequately describe them. The brilliantly colored fabrics used in furnishing Puritan homes were not needed in the meeting houses. None of the pulpits has survived, but since the Puritan ministers were willing enough to use the English pulpits, it is unlikely that the New England carpenters would be instructed to build pulpits in anything but the normal fashion of the times, complete with whatever carvings or turnings their skill could provide. The many instructions for architectural ornament on the meeting houses and the obvious admiration of contemporaries for the more handsome buildings argue against claims that the meeting houses were built in a belligerently doctrinaire spirit of ostentatious austerity.

It is, however, possible to designate these buildings as "Puritan" in another and more basic sense, that of their function. In England the parish churches were sometimes used for village business, the market halls or market places were somtimes used for religious purposes, by Anglicans and Puritans alike, and it was normal for an English town to have both public buildings.

In New England, on the other hand, a town had only one public building for the first quarter of a century, until with the Town House in Boston, 1657, the separation of meeting house functions began. A definitely secular Town House was not provided here until after an increase in population had necessitated a second meeting house (by 1650), with a third coming soon after in 1669. Otherwise the meeting house in each town served both religious and civic purposes and was intended to do so from the beginning.

The meeting houses, built intentionally for a dual purpose

and constructed according to traditional methods, appear to be one of the last phenomena of medieval architecture, and their appearance is all the more remarkable as they were part of striking post-medieval developments in religion and politics. Yet this transformation of English village elements, market hall and post-Reformation parish church, is consistent with the transformation and adaptation of English village practices in the American colonies.[27]

The Puritan contribution to western architecture was not so much in ornament or the lack of it as in a building concept suited to the needs and purposes of the New England theocracy. The theocracy was of short duration. The interior arrangement of the fully developed meeting house survived longer, but it was eventually replaced by orientation along the long rather than the short axis of the building, while an increase in richness of decoration kept pace with that of domestic architecture.

To think of the Puritan settlers as building their meeting houses only as a protest against the English churches in which they had worshipped is to deny them credit for their real accomplishment. To assert that they could solve their building problem only by a weak adaptation of French or Dutch churches is to place too little value on their own creative ability. In order to meet a new communal need, the Puritans devised a new type of public building in which elements of parish church and market hall were used as each community found appropriate. Their purpose was not negative, but positive, and was carried out with not merely Puritan but indeed Yankee ingenuity.

Alphabetical List of Towns

THE FOLLOWING is an alphabetical list of New England towns in which Congregational meeting houses were built between 1632 and 1700. The date, or probable date, of each meeting house is given, together with the documents from which information may be obtained. The dates of the buildings replacing the seventeenth-century meeting houses are also given.

In certain cases the original records are incomplete or lost, and it has been necessary, as noted, to make use of records published as transcriptions or in secondary sources. For a small number of meeting houses it has not been possible to find any records at all, or not enough to insure accurate dating.

For those records which are not paged, entries are designated in the text by date. For full data on published sources, see the Bibliography.

AMESBURY, MASS. FIRST CHURCH.
I, c. 1656. II, 1665. III, 1715.
(Town records, Vol. I, 1656–1717.)

ANDOVER, MASS. FIRST CHURCH.
I, 1661. II, 1708.
(Town records, Vol. I, 1656–1700+. Additional records in Bailey, *Historical sketches of Andover*.)

BARNSTABLE, MASS. CONGREGATIONAL CHURCH.
I, c. 1663. II, 1681. III, 1719.
(Town records, Vol. I, 1641–1713.)

BERWICK, ME. CONGREGATIONAL CHURCH.
I, c. 1659. II, 1797.
(Town records not available before 1701.)

BEVERLY, MASS. FIRST CONGREGATIONAL CHURCH.
  I, c. 1656. II, 1682. III, 1770.
  (Town records, Vol. I, 1665–1685; Vol. II, 1685–1711.)
BOSTON, MASS. FIRST CHURCH.
  I, 1632. II, 1640. III, 1713.
  (*Report of the Record Commissioners of the City of Boston. Second report of the Record Commissioners of the City of Boston.*)
———. SECOND CHURCH.
  I, c. 1650. II, c. 1677. III, 1775.
  (Town records as for Boston, First Church.)
———. THIRD CHURCH.
  I, 1669. II, 1729.
  (Town records as for Boston, First Church.)
———. BRATTLE STREET CHURCH.
  I, 1699. II, 1772.
  (*Records of the church in Brattle Square, Boston.*)
BRAINTREE, MASS. FIRST CHURCH OF CHRIST.
  I, c. 1639. II, 1696. III, 1730.
BRANFORD, CONN. CONGREGATIONAL CHURCH.
  I, c. 1644?. II, 1699. III, 1738.
  (Town records, Vol. I, 1645–1679; Vol. II, 1680–1710.)
BRISTOL, R.I. FIRST CONGREGATIONAL CHURCH.
  I, c. 1684. II, 1795.
  (*Manuel of the First Congregational Church, Bristol.*)
BROOKHAVEN, L.I. FIRST CHURCH.
  I, 1671. II, 1710.
  (*Records of the town of Brookhaven.*)
CAMBRIDGE, MASS. FIRST CONGREGATIONAL CHURCH.
  I, c. 1632. II, 1650. III, 1703.
  (*The records of the town of Cambridge.*)
CHARLESTOWN, MASS. CONGREGATIONAL CHURCH.
  I, c. 1632. II, 1640. III, 1715.
  (Town records, Vol. II, 1629–1661; Vol. III–IV, 1658–1695.)
CHELMSFORD, MASS. FIRST CHURCH.
  I, c. 1655. II, 1710.
  (Records quoted in Allen, *The history of Chelmsford.*)
CLINTON, CONN. CONGREGATIONAL CHURCH.
  I, 1667. II, 1700. III, 1731.
  (Records in *Two hundredth anniversary of the Clinton Congregational Church.*)

CONCORD, MASS. FIRST PARISH CHURCH.
  I, 1636. II, 1668. III, 1712.
  (Town records, Vol. I, 1655–1694; Vol. II, 1694–1733.)
DANBURY, CONN. FIRST CONGREGATIONAL CHURCH.
  I, c. 1684. II, 1696. III, 1785.
  (Town records not available before 1776.)
DANVERS, MASS. FIRST CONGREGATIONAL CHURCH.
  I, 1672. II, 1700. III, 1785.
  (Records in Hanson, *History of the town of Danvers.*)
DEDHAM, MASS. FIRST CHURCH.
  I, 1638. II, 1673. III, 1761.
  (Early records of the town of Dedham, Massachusetts.)
DEERFIELD, MASS. FIRST CHURCH.
  I, before 1673. II, 1682. III, 1694. IV, 1726.
  (Records in Sheldon, *History of Deerfield.*)
DERBY, CONN. FIRST CONGREGATIONAL CHURCH.
  I, 1682. II, 1721.
  (Town records of Derby.)
DORCHESTER, MASS. FIRST CHURCH.
  I, c. 1631. II, 1645. III, 1678. IV, 1743.
  (Dorchester town records.)
DOVER, N.H. FIRST CONGREGATIONAL CHURCH.
  I, c. 1634. II, 1652. III, 1720.
  (Town records, Vol. I, 1647–1753; Vol. II, 1657–1838; Vol.
  III, 1693–1757. Additional records in Scales, *History of Dover.*)
DUNSTABLE, MASS. FIRST CHURCH.
  I, 1674. II, 1683. III, 1732.
  (Records in Fox, *History of the old township of Dunstable.*)
DUXBURY, MASS. CONGREGATIONAL CHURCH.
  I, c. 1638?. II, 1707.
  (Not mentioned in town records.)
EASTHAM, MASS. CONGREGATIONAL CHURCH.
  I, before 1659. II, 1677. III, 1718.
  (Town records, Vol. I, 1654–1745.)
EASTHAMPTON, L.I. FIRST CHURCH.
  I, 1652. II, c. 1682. III, 1717.
  (Records of the town of East-Hampton, Vols. I, II.)
EAST WINDSOR, CONN. FIRST CHURCH.
  I, c. 1695. II, 1710.
  (Records in Stiles, *History of ancient Windsor.*)

ENFIELD, CONN. CONGREGATIONAL CHURCH.
    I, c. 1684. II, 1766.
    (Records in Francis O. Allen, *History of Enfield.*)
ESSEX, MASS. CONGREGATIONAL CHURCH.
    I, 1679. II, 1719.
    (Records in Crowell, *History of the town of Essex.*)
EXETER, N.H. CONGREGATIONAL CHURCH.
    I, c. 1638. II, 1697. III, c. 1730.
    (Town records, Vol. I, 1636–1740. Additional records in Bell, *History of the town of Exeter.*)
FAIRFIELD, CONN. FIRST CONGREGATIONAL CHURCH.
    I, c. 1640. II, 1668. III, 1698. IV, 1779.
    (Town records, 1661–1936.)
FARMINGTON, CONN. FIRST CHURCH OF CHRIST.
    I, before 1672. II, 1709.
    (Town records, Vol. I, 1650–1699.)
FRAMINGHAM, MASS. CONGREGATIONAL CHURCH.
    I, 1700. II, 1735.
    (Records in Barry, *A history of Framingham.*)
GLASTONBURY, CONN. FIRST CONGREGATIONAL CHURCH.
    I, 1693. II, 1735.
    (Town records, 1692–1936. Additional records in Chapin, *Glastonbury for two hundred years.*)
GLOUCESTER, MASS. FIRST CONGREGATIONAL CHURCH.
    I, c. 1643. II, 1660. III, 1698. IV, 1738.
    (Town records, Vol. I, 1642–1694; Vol. II, 1694–1752.)
GREENWICH, CONN. FIRST CONGREGATIONAL CHURCH.
    I, 1695. II, 1730.
    (Town records, 1640–1705.)
GROTON, MASS. FIRST PARISH CHURCH.
    I, 1666. II, 1680. III, 1714.
    (*The early records of Groton.*)
GUILFORD, CONN. FIRST CONGREGATIONAL CHURCH.
    I, c. 1645. II, 1711.
    (Town records, Vol. I, 1645–1700.)
HADDAM, CONN. FIRST CONGREGATIONAL CHURCH.
    I, 1673. II, 1721.
    (Town records, Vol. I, 1666–1700.)
HADLEY, MASS. FIRST CONGREGATIONAL CHURCH.
    I, 1663. II, 1713.

(Town records, Vol. I, 1659–1715.)

HAMPTON, N.H. FIRST CONGREGATIONAL CHURCH.

I, c. 1637. II, 1640. III, 1675. IV, 1719.

(Town records, Vols. I, II, 1645–1832. Additional records in Dow, *History of the town of Hampton.*)

HARTFORD, CONN. FIRST CHURCH OF CHRIST.

I, before 1635. II, c. 1638. III, 1737.

(*Hartford town votes.*)

———. SECOND CHURCH OF CHRIST.

I, before 1673. II, c. 1752.

(Not mentioned in town records.)

HATFIELD, MASS. CONGREGATIONAL CHURCH.

I, 1668. II, 1699. III, 1750.

(Town records, Vol. I, 1660–1672; Vol. II, 1686–1702.)

HAVERHILL, MASS. FIRST CHURCH.

I, 1647. II, 1697. III, 1766.

(Town records, Vol. I, 1643+. Additional records in Chase, *The history of Haverhill.*)

HEMPSTEAD, L.I. FIRST CHURCH.

I, before 1661. II, 1678. III, 1734.

(*Records of the towns of North and South Hempstead.*)

HINGHAM, MASS. CONGREGATIONAL CHURCH.

I, c. 1635. II, 1681.

(Town records, Vol. I, 1635–1700; Vol. II, 1700–1720.)

HUNTINGTON, L.I. FIRST CHURCH.

I, 1665. II, 1717.

(*Huntington town records.*)

IPSWICH, MASS. FIRST CONGREGATIONAL CHURCH.

I, c. 1634. II, 1651. III, 1699. IV, 1846.

(Town records, Vol. I, 1634–1662; Vol. II, 1634–1674; Vol. III, 1696–1720.)

KITTERY, ME. FIRST CONGREGATIONAL CHURCH.

I, before 1669. II, 1671. III, 1727.

(Town records, Vol. I, 1647–1709. Records in Stackpole, *Old Kittery.*)

LANCASTER, MASS. FIRST CHURCH.

I, c. 1658. II, 1685. III, 1704.

(*The early records of Lancaster.*)

LEXINGTON, MASS. FIRST PARISH CHURCH.

I, 1692. II, 1713.

(*Report of a committee . . . of Lexington.*)

LYME, CONN. FIRST CONGREGATIONAL CHURCH.
   I, before 1673. II, 1687. III, 1735.
   (Town records, 1665–1936.)

LYNN, MASS. FIRST CONGREGATIONAL CHURCH.
   I, c. 1632. II, 1682. III, 1827.
   (Town records not available.)

MALDEN, MASS. FIRST CONGREGATIONAL CHURCH.
   I, 1649. II, 1658. III, 1727.
   (Town records, Vol. I, 1678–1764.)

MANCHESTER, MASS. FIRST CHURCH.
   I, 1672. II, 1692. III, 1720.
   (*Town records of Manchester,* Vol. I, 1636–1736.)

MARBLEHEAD, MASS. FIRST CONGREGATIONAL CHURCH.
   I, c. 1639?. II, 1715.
   ("Marblehead Town Records.")

MARLBOROUGH, MASS. FIRST CONGREGATIONAL CHURCH.
   I, before 1663. II, 1688. III, 1808.
   (Town records, Vol. I, 1666–1698.)

MARSHFIELD, MASS. FIRST CONGREGATIONAL CHURCH.
   I, before 1652. II, 1657. III, 1706.
   (Town records, Vol. I, 1643–1803. Records in Richards, *History of Marshfield.*)

MEDFIELD, MASS. FIRST CHURCH.
   I, 1654. II, 1706.
   (Town records, Vol. I, 1649–1755. Records in Tilden, *History of the town of Medfield.*)

MEDFORD, MASS. FIRST CHURCH.
   I, 1695. II, 1726.
   (Town records, Vol. I, 1675–1718.)

MENDON, MASS. FIRST CHURCH.
   I, 1668. II, 1680. III, 1690. IV, 1733.
   (Records in Metcalf, *Annals of the town of Mendon.*)

MIDDLEBORO, MASS. FIRST CONGREGATIONAL CHURCH.
   I, c. 1675? II, 1700. III, c. 1744.
   (Town records, Vol. I, 1658–1705.)

MIDDLETOWN, CONN. FIRST CONGREGATIONAL CHURCH.
   I, 1653. II, 1670. III, 1715.
   (Town records, Vol. I, 1652–1735.)

MILFORD, CONN. CHURCH OF CHRIST.

I, 1641. II, 1728.

(Town records, Vol. I, 1696+.)

MILTON, MASS. FIRST CONGREGATIONAL CHURCH.

I, c. 1664. II, 1671. III, 1727.

(*Milton town records.*)

NASHUA, N.H. FIRST CONGREGATIONAL CHURCH.

I, after 1685. II, 1738.

(Not mentioned in town records.)

NEWBURY, MASS. FIRST CONGREGATIONAL CHURCH.

I, c. 1635. II, 1646. III, 1661. IV, 1699. V, 1766.

(Town records, Vol. I, 1637+. Additional records in Coffin, *A sketch of the history of Newbury.*)

NEW HAVEN, CONN. FIRST CHURCH OF CHRIST.

I, 1640. II, 1669. III, 1754.

(*Records of the colony and plantation of New Haven, from 1638 to 1649. Records of the colony or jurisdiction of New Haven, from May, 1653, to the Union. New Haven town records.*)

NEW LONDON, CONN. FIRST CONGREGATIONAL CHURCH.

I, 1652. II, 1682. III, 1694. IV, 1785.

(Town records, Vol. I, 1647–1666; Vol. II, 1666–1703. Records in Caulkins, *History of New London.*)

NEWPORT, R.I. FIRST CONGREGATIONAL CHURCH.

I, 1698. II, 1729.

(Town records not available.)

NEWTON, MASS. FIRST CONGREGATIONAL CHURCH.

I, 1659. II, 1696. III, 1721.

(Town records, Vol. I, 1679–1748.)

NORTHAMPTON, MASS. FIRST CONGREGATIONAL CHURCH.

I, 1655. II, 1662. III, 1736.

(Town records, Vol. I, 1654–1754.)

NORWALK, CONN. FIRST CONGREGATIONAL CHURCH.

I, 1657. II, 1679. III, 1720.

(Town records, Vol. I, 1653–1707.)

NORWICH, CONN. FIRST CONGREGATIONAL CHURCH.

I, before 1668. II, 1673. III, 1712.

(Town records, Vol. I, 1670+. Records in Caulkins, *History of Norwich,* and in Kelly, *Early Connecticut meetinghouses.*)

OYSTER RIVER, N.H. CONGREGATIONAL CHURCH.

I, 1656. II, 1712–13.

(Records in Scales, *History of Dover.*)

PLYMOUTH, MASS. CONGREGATIONAL CHURCH.
I, 1648. II, 1683. III, 1744.
(Records of the town of Plymouth.)

PORTSMOUTH, N.H. CONGREGATIONAL CHURCH.
I, c. 1640. II, 1657. III, 1712.
(Portsmouth records.)

PORTSMOUTH, R.I. CONGREGATIONAL CHURCH.
I, 1639. Congregation not permanent.
(Records of the colony of Rhode Island and Providence plantations.)

PRESTON, CONN. CONGREGATIONAL CHURCH.
I, 1698. II, 1739.
(Town records, Vol. I, 1688–1705.)

QUABAUG, MASS. FIRST CONGREGATIONAL CHURCH.
I, c. 1664. II, 1715.
(Records in Josiah H. Temple, *History of North Brookfield.*)

READING, MASS. CONGREGATIONAL CHURCH.
I, c. 1644?. II, c. 1689. III, 1752.
(Town records, Vol. I, 1644–1773.)

REHOBOTH, MASS. FIRST CHURCH.
I, 1644. II, 1674. III, 1716.
(Records in Tilton, *A history of Rehoboth.*)

ROWLEY, MASS. FIRST CONGREGATIONAL CHURCH.
I, c. 1639. II, 1697. III, 1749.
(Town records, Vol. I, 1660–1712.)

ROXBURY, MASS. FIRST CONGREGATIONAL CHURCH.
I, c. 1632?. II, 1674. III, 1741.
(Town records, Vol. I, 1648–1730.)

SALEM, MASS. CONGREGATIONAL CHURCH.
I, c. 1635. II, 1670. III, 1718.
(Town records of Salem, Vol. I, 1634–1659; Vol. II, 1659–1680; Vol. III, 1680–1691.)

SALISBURY, MASS. CONGREGATIONAL CHURCH.
I, c. 1640. II, 1714.
(Records in Joseph Merrill, *History of Amesbury.*)

SAYBROOK, CONN. FIRST CONGREGATIONAL CHURCH.
I, before 1640. II, 1678. III, 1726.
(Town records, Vol. I, 1667–1727.)

SCITUATE, MASS. FIRST CONGREGATIONAL CHURCH.

I, c. 1635. II, 1682. III, 1707.
(Town records, Vol. I, 1649–1707.)
SIMSBURY, CONN. FIRST CHURCH OF CHRIST.
I, 1683. II, 1740.
(Town records, Vol. I, 1660–1691.)
SOUTHAMPTON, L.I. FIRST CHURCH.
I, c. 1645. II, 1651. III, 1707.
(*The first book of records of the town of Southampton. The second book of records of the town of Southampton.*)
SOUTHOLD, L.I. FIRST CHURCH.
I, c. 1640. II, 1683. III, c. 1710.
(Records in Whitaker, *Whitaker's Southold.*)
SPRINGFIELD, MASS. FIRST CONGREGATIONAL CHURCH.
I, 1645. II, 1677. III, 1749.
(Records in Burt, *The first century of the history of Springfield.*)
STAMFORD, CONN. FIRST CONGREGATIONAL CHURCH.
I, c. 1640. II, 1671. III, 1703.
(Town Records, Vols. I, II, 1630–1806.)
STONINGTON, CONN. FIRST CONGREGATIONAL CHURCH.
I, 1661. II, 1672. III, 1729.
(Town records, Vol. I, 1660–1672; Vol. II, 1651–1714.)
STRATFORD, CONN. FIRST CONGREGATIONAL CHURCH.
I, before 1661. II, 1680. III, 1743.
(Town records, Vol. I, 1652–1680.)
SUDBURY, MASS. CONGREGATIONAL CHURCH.
I, 1643. II, 1653. III, 1687. IV, 1724.
(Town records, Vol. I, 1638–1706.)
SUFFIELD, CONN. FIRST CONGREGATIONAL CHURCH.
I, 1699. II, 1749.
(Town records, Vol. I, 1670–1712.)
SWANSEA, MASS. FIRST CONGREGATIONAL CHURCH.
I, 1679. II, 1778.
(Town records, Vol. I, 1670–1705.)
TAUNTON, MASS. FIRST CHURCH.
I, before 1656. II, 1726.
(Not mentioned in town records.)
TOPSFIELD, MASS. FIRST CONGREGATIONAL CHURCH.
I, before 1658. II, 1663. III, 1703.
(*Town records of Topsfield, Massachusetts.*)

WALLINGFORD, CONN. FIRST CONGREGATIONAL CHURCH.
  I, 1678. II, 1717.
  (Records in Davis, *History of Wallingford.*)
WATERBURY, CONN. FIRST CONGREGATIONAL CHURCH.
  I, 1692. II, 1796.
  (Records in Anderson, *The town and city of Waterbury.*)
WATERTOWN, MASS. FIRST CONGREGATIONAL CHURCH.
  I, c. 1635?. II, 1656. III, 1695. IV, 1723.
  (*Watertown records,* Vols. I, II.)
WELLS, ME. FIRST CONGREGATIONAL CHURCH.
  I, before 1664?. II, 1699. III, 1767.
  (Records in Bourne, *History of Wells and Kennebunk.*)
WENHAM, MASS. FIRST CONGREGATIONAL CHURCH.
  I, c. 1642. II, 1688. III, 1748.
  (*Wenham town records.*)
WESTFIELD, MASS. FIRST CONGREGATIONAL CHURCH.
  I, 1672. II, c. 1720.
  (Records in Lockwood, *Westfield and its historic influences.*)
WETHERSFIELD, CONN. FIRST CHURCH OF CHRIST.
  I, c. 1647. II, 1686. III, 1762.
  (Town records, Vol. I, 1646–1783.)
WEYMOUTH, MASS. FIRST CHURCH.
  I, c. 1635. II, 1682. III, 1751.
  (Town records, Vol. I, 1635–1772.)
WINDSOR, CONN. FIRST CHURCH.
  I, c. 1639. II, 1686. III, 1757.
  (Town records, Vol. I, 1650–1714.)
WOBURN, MASS. FIRST CONGREGATIONAL CHURCH.
  I, c. 1642. I, 1672. III, 1752.
  (Records in Sewall, *History of Woburn.*)
WOODBURY, CONN. FIRST CONGREGATIONAL CHURCH.
  I, 1681. II, 1746.
  (Not mentioned in town records.)
WOODSTOCK, CONN. FIRST CONGREGATIONAL CHURCH.
  I, 1694. II, 1720.
  (Town records, Vol. I, 1686–1721.)
WRENTHAM, MASS. CONGREGATIONAL CHURCH.
  I, 1682. II, 18th century.
  (Town records, Vol. I, 1660–1829.)
YARMOUTH, MASS. FIRST CONGREGATIONAL CHURCH.

I, c. 1640. II, 1683. III, 1716.
(Town records, Vol. I, 1677–1778.)
YORK, ME. CONGREGATIONAL CHURCH.
    I, c. 1636. II, 1667. III, 1712.
    (Records in Banks, *History of York*.)

Chronological List of
Meeting Houses, 1631–1700

THE FOLLOWING meeting houses were built in New England from 1631 to 1700. The dates are based on the records listed in Appendix A, which are not in all cases complete. Some of the dates given here are therefore probable rather than certain.

Some of the more important information about the buildings is included here, such as the names of carpenters, dimensions, shapes, materials, and dates of installation of galleries and pews. The records may be consulted for additional details. The meeting houses are listed alphabetically within each year.

1631 —— Dorchester, Mass., I (about).
　　　　Thatched. Stairs and loft, 1634.
1632 —— Boston, Mass. First Church, I.
　　　　Cambridge, Mass., I (about).
　　　　　Square.
　　　　Charlestown, Mass., I (about).
　　　　Lynn, Mass., I (about).
　　　　　Turret by 1660.
　　　　Roxbury, Mass., I (about).
　　　　　Rectangular. Ends clapboarded, 1656. Galleries, turret, gable ends, 1659.
1633 —— Gloucester, Mass., I (about?).
1634 —— Dover, N.H., I (about?).
　　　　Ipswich, Mass., I (about).
　　　　　Gallery, 1643.
1635 —— Hartford, Conn. First Church, I (before).

Hingham, Mass., I (about).
    Gallery on north, posts and pillars turned, 1644.
Newbury, Mass., I (about).
Salem, Mass., I (about).
    Daubed, 1637. Enlarged 25', 1639. Chimney.
Scituate, Mass., I (about?).
Watertown, Mass., I (about?).
    Gallery, 1649. Turret, 1651.
Weymouth, Mass., I (about).
    Three galleries, 1667. Shingled, 1672.

1636 —— Concord, Mass., I.
York, Me., I (about).

1637 —— Hampton, N.H., I (about?).

1638 —— Dedham, Mass., I.
    36' x 20' x 12'. Thatched, later shingled. Belfry.
Duxbury, Mass., I (about?).
Exeter, N.H., I (about).
Hartford, Conn. First Church, II (about).
    Clapboards, porch. Galleries, 1644, 1660.

1639 —— Braintree, Mass., I (about).
Marblehead, Mass., I (about?).
    40' long. Gallery, 1662–63. Turret by 1663.
    Enlarged 12', 1672.
Portsmouth, R.I., I.
Rowley, Mass., I (about).
Windsor, Conn., I (about).
    Seated, 1655. "Lanthorn" by 1658.

1640 —— Boston, Mass. First Church, II.
    Rectangular. Clapboards, shingles. Galleries by 1675.
    Platform by 1699.
Charlestown, Mass., II.
Fairfield, Conn., I (about).
Hampton, N.H., II.
    Richard Knight, carpenter. 40' x 22' x 13'. West gallery,
    1649.
New Haven, Conn., I.
    William Andrews, carpenter. 50' x 50'. Seated, 1645.
    Banisters, rails, platform by 1658. Turret.
Portsmouth, N.H., I (about).
Salisbury, Mass., I (about).
    Bell hung, 1644. Enlarged 12', 1652.

Saybrook, Conn., I (about).
    40′ x 30′.
Southold, L.I., I (about).
Stamford, Conn., I (about).
Yarmouth, Mass., I (about).
1641 —— Milford, Conn., I.
    30′ x 30′. Gallery by 1696. Turret by 1718.
1642 —— Wenham, Mass., I (about).
    Rectangular. Ends plastered, 1662. Galleries, 1674, 1682.
Woburn, Mass., I (about).
1643 —— Gloucester, Mass., II (about).
    Rectangular. Galleries at ends, 1686–91.
Sudbury, Mass., I.
    John Rutter, carpenter. 30′ x 20′ x 8′.
1644 —— Branford, Conn., I (about?).
Reading, Mass., I (about?).
    Rectangular. Gallery on south side, 1657.
Rehoboth, Mass., I.
    Rectangular. Enlarged 1659.
1645 —— Dorchester, Mass., II.
    Gallery, 1645. Shutters, 1662. Table, 1667. Bell frame detached. Clapboarded.
Guilford, Conn., I (about).
    Rectangular. West gallery, 1668. East gallery, 1679.
Southampton, L.I., I (about).
    Heated.
Springfield, Mass., I.
    Thomas Cooper, carpenter. 45′ x 25′ x 9′. Galleries and two turrets, 1661.
1646 —— Ipswich, Mass., II.
    George Norton, carpenter. Turret. Clapboards.
    Galleries. Cross-gabled?
Newbury, Mass., II.
1647 —— Haverhill, Mass., I.
    Thomas Davis, carpenter. Enlarged, 1659. Gallery, 1667.
Wethersfield, Conn., I (about).
    Clapboards, wainscot. Galleries, 1683.
1648 —— Plymouth, Mass., I.
1649 —— Malden, Mass. I.
1650 —— Boston, Mass. Second Church, I (about).

Cambridge, Mass., II.

40′ x 40′. South gallery, 1660. North gallery, 1673.

1651 —— Southampton, L.I., II.

Ellis Post, Richard Post, carpenters. 30′ x 24′ x 8½′.
Galleries, c. 1682.

1652 —— Dover, N.H., II.

Richard Waldern, carpenter. 40′ x 26′ x 16′. Turret,
1665.

Easthampton, L.I., I.

26′ x 20′ x 8′. Thatched. Gallery, 1682.

Marshfield, Mass., I (before).

New London, Conn., I.

John Elderkin, carpenter.

1653 —— Barnstable, Mass., I (about).

Middletown, Conn., I.

20′ x 20′ x 10′. Gallery, 1665.

Sudbury, Mass., II.

Peter King, Thomas Plympton, carpenters. 40′ x 24′
(?) x 12′. Clapboarded. Two front gables.

1654 —— Medfield, Mass., I.

Gallery, thatched. Bell separate. Seated, 1658.

1655 —— Chelmsford, Mass., I (about).

Bell, 1680.

Northampton, Mass., II.

1656 —— Amesbury, Mass., I (about).

Beverly, Mass., I (about).

Gallery on north. East gallery and turret, 1671.

Oyster River, N.H., I.

Valentine Hill, carpenter.

Taunton, Mass., I (before).

Watertown, Mass., II.

John Sherman, carpenter. 40′ x 40′. Platform. Galleries,
1679.

1657 —— Marshfield, Mass., II.

Ensign Eames, William Macomber, carpenters.

Norwalk, Conn., I.

30′ x 18′. Clapboards, shingles. Set on posts?

Portsmouth, N.H., II.

40′ x 40′ x 16′.

1658 —— Lancaster, Mass., I (about).

Malden, Mass., II.

Job Lane, carpenter. 33′ x 33′ x 16′. Turret. Galleries by 1684.

Topsfield, Mass., I (before).

1659 —— Berwick, Me., I (about).

Eastham, L.I., I (before).

Newton, Mass., I.

1661 —— Andover, Mass., I.

Shingled. Galleries by 1690's.

Hempstead, L.I., I (before).

Newbury, Mass., III.

Henry Jaques, carpenter. Rectangular. Gallery. Porch for stairs.

Stonington, Conn., I.

Thomas Minor, Thomas Park, carpenters.

Stratford, Conn., I (before).

Gallery. Porch for stairs.

1662 —— Northampton, Mass., II.

42′ x 42′. Galleries, 1670, 1680.

1663 —— Hadley, Mass., I.

45′ x 24′, with 6′ lean-to on each side. North and south galleries, 1698.

Marlborough, Mass., I (before).

Thatched. Gallery.

Topsfield, Mass., II.

Rectangular. Gallery "on length," and pulpit, 1681. West gallery, 1682. East gallery, 1694.

1664 —— Milton, Mass., I (about).

Quabaug, Mass., I (about).

Wells, Me., I (before?).

1665 —— Amesbury, Mass., II.

30′ x 25′ x 16′. Family pew on outside, 1696. Galleries, 1699.

Huntington, L.I., I.

Rectangular. East and north galleries, 1707.

1666 —— Groton, Mass., I.

Thatched. Gallery. Two doors. Two stairs.

1667 —— Clinton, Conn., I.

York, Me., II.

Henry Sayward, carpenter. 28′ wide, 16′ high. Turret. Balusters. Galleries, 1680.

1668 —— Concord, Mass., II.
        Fairfield, Conn., II.
        Hatfield, Mass., I.
           30′ x 30′. Turret. Gallery. Dormers, 1688.
        Mendon, Mass., I.
        Norwich, Conn., I (before).
1669 —— Boston, Mass. Third Church, I.
           Robert Tweld, carpenter. 75′ x 57′. Three porches.
        Kittery, Me., I (before).
        New Haven, Conn., II.
           Nathan Andrews, carpenter. 55′ x 35′ (?). Galleries.
           Turret.
1670 —— Middletown, Conn., II.
           John Hull, carpenter. 32′ x 32′ x 15′. Gallery, 1676.
        Salem, Mass., II.
           60′ x 50′ x 20′. Turret. Chimney. East and west galleries.
           North gallery, 1688.
1671 —— Brookhaven, L.I., I.
           Nathaniel Morton, carpenter. 28′ x 28′ x 10′.
        Kittery, Me., II.
        Milton, Mass., II.
        Stamford, Conn., II.
           38′ x 38′. Platform and turret.
1672 —— Danvers, Mass., I.
           34′ x 28′ x 16′. Two galleries, 1684.
        Farmington, Conn., I (before).
        Manchester, Mass., I.
           18′ high. Rectangular. "Two Gable Ends."
        Stonington, Conn., II.
           Thomas Minor, Thomas Park, carpenters. 40′ x 22′ x
           14′. Gallery.
        Westfield, Mass., I.
           36′ x 36′. Turret. Galleries, 1703.
        Woburn, Mass., I.
           Turret. Gallery.
1673 —— Dedham, Mass., II.
           John Baker, Daniel Pond, carpenters. 38′ x 24′–26′.
           North and east galleries. Enlarged, 1702.
        Deerfield, Mass., I (before).
        Haddam, Conn., I.

John Clarke, carpenter. 28′ x 24′ x 13′. "Pyramids."

Hartford, Conn. Second Church, I (before).

Lyme, Conn., I (before).

Norwich, Conn., II.

John Elderkin, carpenter. Gallery. Enlarged, 1689. "Pyramids."

1674 —— Dunstable, Mass., I.

Rectangular.

Rehoboth, Mass., II.

Rectangular. Front and side galleries.

Roxbury, Mass., II.

Galleries, 1683.

1675 —— Hampton, N.H., III.

Middleboro, Mass., I (about?).

1677 —— Boston, Mass. Second Church, II (about).

Eastham, Mass., II.

Belfry, 1681.

Springfield, Mass., II.

John Allis, carpenter. 50′ x 40′. Clapboards and shingles. Turret.

1678 —— Dorchester, Mass., III.

Bell separate.

Hempstead, L.I., II.

Joseph Carpenter, carpenter. 30′ x 24′ x 12′. Lean-to on each side.

Saybrook, Conn., II.

William Bushnell, carpenter. Cedar clapboards.

Wallingford, Conn., I.

28′ x 24′ x 10′. Pulpit moved to west wall, 1691.

1679 —— Essex, Mass., I.

Norwalk, Conn., II.

40′ x 40′ x 16′.

Swansea, Mass., I.

40′ x 22′ x 16′.

1680 —— Groton, Mass., II.

Mendon, Mass., II.

Samuel Hayward, carpenter. 26′ x 24′ x 16′.

Stratford, Conn., II.

48′ x 42′ x 16′. Galleries later. Porch.

1681 —— Barnstable, Mass., II.

Hingham, Mass., II.

55′ x 45′ x 21′. Galleries. Enlarged, 1730, 1755.

Woodbury, Conn., I.

1682 —— Beverly, Mass., II.

50′ x 40′. West and south galleries. Belfry.

Deerfield, Mass., II.

Derby, Conn., I.

John Hull, carpenter. 28′ 20′ x 10′. Transom windows. Banisters on seats.

Easthampton, L.I., II.

Lynn, Mass., II.

50′ x 44′(?). Galleries, balustrades.

New London, Conn., II.

John Elderkin, carpenter. 40′ x 40′ x 20′. Four gables with "pyramids." Turret. Galleries.

Scituate, Mass., II.

Weymouth, Mass., II.

Jacob Nash, carpenter. 45′ x 40′ x 20′. Four gables and platform. Galleries.

Wrentham, Mass., I.

36′ x 26′ x 16′. Gallery, 1684.

1683 —— Dunstable, Mass., II.

Plymouth, Mass., II.

45′ x 40′ x 16′.

Simsbury, Conn., I.

Thomas Barber, carpenter. 25′ x 24′ x 14′. Gallery, 1690. Clapboards and shingles. "Pyramids."

Southold, L.I., II.

Yarmouth, Mass., II.

Seat over men's door, 1687. Gallery "above great window," 1691.

1684 —— Bristol, R.I., I (about).

Danbury, Conn., I (about).

Enfield, Conn., I (about).

1685 —— Lancaster, Mass., II.

Nashua, N.H., I (after).

1686 —— Wethersfield, Conn., II.

50′ x 50′. Dormer windows.

Windsor, Conn., II.

50′ x 40′.

1687 —— Lyme, Conn., II.

40′ x 20′ x 16½′. Cedar shingles. Galleries, 1702.
Sudbury, Mass., III.
    Daniel Pond, carpenter. 38′ x 24′–26′.
1688 —— Marlborough, Mass., II.
    John Newton, Moses Newton, carpenters, 40′ x 30′ x 16′.
    Wenham, Mass., II.
        Rectangular. Gallery. Bell, 1694.
1689 —— Reading, Mass., II.
    Enlarged, 1701. Pulpit moved to east side, 1717.
1690 —— Mendon, Mass., III.
    John Andruse, carpenter. 30′ x 30′ x 16′.
1692 —— Lexington, Mass., I.
    Manchester, Mass., II.
        30′ x 25′ x 16′. Three galleries.
    Waterbury, Conn., I.
1693 —— Glastonbury, Conn., I.
    Voted to enlarge by galleries or lean-to, 1696.
1694 —— Deerfield, Mass., III.
        30′ x 30′. Galleries.
    New London, Conn., III.
    Woodstock, Conn., I.
        John Holmes, carpenter. 30′ x 26′ x 14′. One gable on
    each side.
1695 —— East Windsor, Conn., I (about).
    Greenwich, Conn., I.
        32′ x 26′ x 16′. Clapboards and shingles.
    Medford, Mass., I.
        30′ x 27′ x 16′. Gallery. Shingled.
    Watertown, Mass., III.
1696 —— Braintree, Mass., II.
    Stone. Platform, 1714.
    Danbury, Conn., II.
    Newton, Mass., II.
    John Brewer, carpenter. Turret. Weathervane, 1698.
1697 —— Exeter, N.H., II.
    Haverhill, Mass., II.
        John Haseltine, carpenter. 50′ x 42′ x 18′. Galleries.
    Turret.
    Rowley, Mass., II.
        50′ x 40′ x 18′.

1698 —— Fairfield, Conn., III.

    50′ x 55′(?).

   Gloucester, Mass., III.

    40′ x 40′ x 16′.

   Newport, R.I., I.

   Preston, Conn., I.

    35′ x 25′ x 16′. Gallery.

1699 —— Boston, Mass. Brattle Street Church, I.

    72′ x 52′. Upper gallery.

   Branford, Conn., II.

    Daniel Clark, carpenter. Square. Turret.

   Hatfield, Mass., II.

    45′ x 45′. Four gable windows.

   Ipswich, Mass., III.

    66′ x 60′ x 26′. Galleries. Belfry, 1712.

   Newbury, Mass., IV.

    Stephen Jaques, carpenter. 24′ high. Turret.

   Suffield, Conn., I.

    40′ x 40′. Galleries.

   Wells, Me., II.

    Galleries, 1714. Tower, 1719.

1700 —— Clinton, Conn., II.

    35′ x 35′. Galleries, 1712.

   Danvers, Mass., II.

    48′ x 42′ x 20′.

   Framingham, Mass., I.

    Rectangular. Enlarged to square, 1715.

   Middleboro, Mass., II.

    36′ x 30′ x 16′.

Notes

Abbreviations

B. H. P.: *Bulletin de la Société de l'Histoire du Protestantisme Français*

C. J.: *Journal of the House of Commons*

CAL. S. P. COL.: *Calendar of State Papers, Colonial Series*

CAL. S. P. DOM.: *Calendar of State Papers, Domestic Series*

L. J.: *Journal of the House of Lords*

M. B. C. RECORDS: *Records of the Governor and Company of the Massachusetts Bay in New England* (Boston, 1853)

M. H. S. COLLS.: *Collections of the Massachusetts Historical Society*

R. C. H. M.: *Royal Commission on the Ancient and Historical Monuments and Constructions of England*

V. C. H.: *Victoria History of the Counties of England*

For full data about the other works cited in the notes, see the Bibliography.

CHAPTER ONE: *New England Meeting Houses of the Great Migration, 1630–1642*

1. Rowse, *The Elizabethans and America,* pp. 89–123, 159–187.
2. Quoted in Thornton, *The landing at Cape Ann,* p. 32.
3. Rose-Troup, *The Massachusetts Bay Company and its predecessors,* p. 13.
4. *The acts and ordinances of the Eastland Company,* Series 3, XI, pp. 142–15.
5. Hill, *An historical account of the plantation in Ulster,* p. 88.
6. *Ibid.,* p. 223.
7. Phillips, *Londonderry and the London Companies 1609–1629,* p. 14.
8. *The three charters of the Virginia Company of London,* pp. 73, 99.

9. Eburne, *A plain pathway to plantations,* p. 97.

10. *Cal. S. P. Col.,* I, p. 88. Further grant of incorporation as Governor and Company of the Massachusetts Bay in New England was made February 27, 1628/29 (*ibid.,* p. 96).

11. *M. B. C. Records,* I, pp. 3–20; also *Cal. S. P. Col.,* I, p. 97.

12. *M. B. C. Records,* I, p. 55

13. *Ibid.,* p. 68.

14. *Ibid.,* p. 389.

15. Winthrop, *Journal,* I, p. 75.

16. *Ibid.,* p. 89.

17. Rose-Troup, *John White,* p. 105.

18. Thornton, *op. cit.,* pp. 79 ff. For the alleged new location of the Governor's house in Salem, see Phippen, "The 'Old Planters' of Salem. . . . ," p. 104: "The Governor's house, which was first set up at Cape Ann, in 1624, by the party who went over from Plymouth with Edward Winslow, was shaken and brought to Naumkeag, and re-erected here, a few rods from the water, upon the elevated banks of the North River, now the northeast corner of Washington and Church streets, — the Newhall house there standing being in part the same."

19. *M. B. C. Records,* I, p. 386.

20. Higginson, "New Englands plantation," p. 123.

21. *Cal. S. P. Col.,* VIII, p. 194.

22. Roger Clap, *Memoirs* (Boston, 1731), in Young, *Chronicles of the first planters of the colony of Massachusetts Bay,* p. 351.

23. Mather, *Magnalia Christi Americana,* I, p. 79.

24. *M. B. C. Records,* I, p. 73.

25. Bartlett, *An historical sketch of Charlestown,* p. 5.

26. Quoted in Frothingham, *History of Charlestown, Massachusetts,* p. 55.

27. *Ibid.,* p. 66.

28. *M. B. C. Records,* I, p. 75.

29. Winthrop, *Journal,* I, p. 60.

30. *Ibid.,* p. 89.

31. *Seventh Report of the Royal Commission on Historical Manuscripts,* p. 547.

32. *T.R.:* Town Records. —— As indicated in the Preface, the records of the New England towns are the most extensive source of information about the meeting houses. In order to reduce the bulk of notes, references to these records are noted in the text, as is done

here for Watertown. The manuscripts or printed transcriptions to which the page numbers refer are identified in Appendix A, which is arranged alphabetically by town.

33. Hubbard, *A general history of New England,* p. 220. For English examples of a minister's house with chapel attached, see the Chapel of St. Mary at Great Horkesley (Figure 16) and the Black Chapel at Great Waltham, both fifteenth-century buildings in Essex.

34. Waddington, *Surrey Congregational history,* p. 290: John Lothrop, who succeeded Henry Jacob as pastor of the church in Southwark, escaped to Scituate, Mass., in 1634 with thirty members of his congregation. "An original letter, still in existence, reports their arrival, and describes their first meeting, held at the house of Mr. Cudworth."

35. Calder, *The New Haven colony,* p. 90. The use of private houses indicated here is not documented but reported from tradition.

36. Winthrop, *Journal,* I, p. 318. The 1640 meeting house lasted a remarkably long time, until it was destroyed by fire in 1711. "Indeed, considering the place where the House stood, and the Circumstances of the Building about it; 'tis a great wonder of Gods merciful Providence, that it stood so long as it did." (Wadsworth, *Five Sermons,* p. 75.)

37. Orcutt, *Good old Dorchester,* p. 224.

38. Edward Johnson, *A History of New-England,* p. 45.

39. The length of the Marblehead meeting house is established by the town vote of April 6, 1672: "Its agred by generall Consent that a Lentoe shall be built adiyning toe the backside of the meeting house twelve foote in bredth: fortie foot in Lengthh: with three gabell ends in the same of timbr work" (*T.R.,* 263). Hampton may have been another town in which meetings were first held in a house, according to the Colony Records for March 3, 1635/36: "Ordered, that there shalbe a plantacon setled at Wenicunnet [Hampton] & that Mr Dumer & Mr Spencer shall have power to presse men to build a howse forthwth, in some convenient place" (*M. B. C. Records,* I, p. 167).

40. *New England Weekly Journal,* April 28, 1729, quoted in Ayer, "The South Meeting House, Boston," p. 266.

41. Lechford, "Plain dealing: or newes from New-England," p. 76.

42. Cotton, *The way of the churches of Christ in New-England,* pp. 68–69.

43. Lechford, *op. cit.*, p. 82.
44. *M. B. C. Records*, I, p. 157.
45. *Ibid.*, pp. 181, 291.
46. *Ibid.*, pp. 267, 284, 311.
47. Shattuck, *A history of the town of Concord*, p. 7.
48. *Ibid.*, p. 9.
49. *Winthrop Papers*, III, pp. 181–82.
50. Phillips, *op. cit.*, p. 15.
51. *Ibid.*, Plate 3, f. p. 12.
52. *M. B. C. Records*, I, pp. 166–67.
53. Willsford, *Architectonice*, p. 13.
54. *Ibid.*
55. Leybourn, *A platform for purchasers*, p. 113.

CHAPTER TWO: *Continental Protestant Architecture Before 1630*

1. See particularly Garvan, "The Protestant plain style before 1630"; Coolidge, "Hingham builds a meetinghouse"; Overby, "Architecture and the Protestant community"; and Sinnott, *Meetinghouse & church in early New England, passim*.
2. Lewy, *Schloss Hartenfels bei Torgau*, pp. 85–87.
3. See also the chapel of Moritzburg bei Halle by Nicholas Hofmann, 1509 (*ibid.*, p. 84).
4. Kerr, *A compend of Luther's theology*, p. 146.
5. Kidd, *Documents illustrative of the Continental Reformation*, p. 199.
6. *Luther's works*, LI, p. 333.
7. Drummond, *Church architecture of Protestantism*, p. 29.
8. Merz, "Joseph Furttenbach," pp. 115–22.
9. Maxwell, *An outline of Christian worship*, p. 80.
10. *Ibid.*, pp. 83–84.
11. *Ibid.*, p. 119.
12. Baird, *History of the rise of the Huguenots of France*, I, pp. 294–95, 335.
13. *Ibid.*, p. 560.
14. Haag, eds., *La France protestante*, I, p. 49.
15. *Ibid.*, X, pp. 62–63.
16. *Ibid.*, pp. 92–97.
17. *Ibid.*, p. 234.
18. Steyert, *Nouvelle histoire de Lyon*, III, p. 143.
19. Communication from A. Joly, Archivist, Bibliothèque de la

Ville de Lyon, February 22, 1963.

20. *B. H. P.*, 88 (1939), p. 4.
21. *Ibid.*, 40 (1891), p. 204.
22. *Ibid.*, 44 (1895), p. 368.
23. *Ibid.*, 36 (1887), p. 221.
24. *Ibid.*, 63–64 (1914–15), p. 36.
25. *Ibid.*, 83 (1934), p. 347.
26. Hamberg, *Tempelbygge för Protestanter*, pp. 29–41.
27. Perret, *Des fortifications et artifices,* German edition, Book II, Plates H, X.
28. Rectangular "temples" were apparently built at Dieppe (1600), Charmont (1601), Bègles (1604), Charenton (1606 and a second building of 1623), Villeneuve-La Rochelle (1630), Montegnac-sur-Charente (1634), and Mer (date uncertain). A square temple was built at Anduze, and a twelve-sided one at Petit-Quevilly in 1599. Octagonal plans were used at Caen (1611–1612), Montauban (1615), and Rouen (date uncertain). See *B. H. P., passim;* Félice, *Les protestants d'autrefois;* and Pannier, *L'église réformée de Paris sous Henry IV,* for fragmentary descriptions of these buildings.
29. Félice, *op. cit.*, I, pp. 3–37.
30. Pannier, *Salomon de Brosse*, pp. 86–90, 235–40.
31. Hautecoeur, *Histoire de l'architecture classique en France*, I², p. 714. A Vitruvian source for the Charenton Temple was proposed by L. Vaudoyer in the *Magasin pittoresque,* 1845, p. 77. The basilica at Fano was 60 feet wide and 120 feet long. In the Barbaro edition of Vitruvius another basilica is illustrated with shorter and broader proportions closer to those of the Charenton Temple (Vitruvius Pollio, *De architectura libri decem,* pp. 166–67). De Brosse's choice of the basilical plan for a Protestant church may have been influenced by Alberti's remark that a preacher's voice might be better heard in a wooden-roofed basilica than in a stone-vaulted temple (Alberti, *I dieci libri de l'architettura,* p. 143v.).
32. Vermeulen, *Handboek tot de Geschiednis der Nederlandsche bouwkunst,* III, pp. 368–69.
33. Such interiors are well illustrated in the paintings of de Witte and Saenredam.
34. Vermeulen, *op. cit.*, II, pp. 363–64, Plan Figure 269, Plates 617, 624.

35. *Ibid.*, I, p. 364 n.
36. *Ibid.*, II, p. 366, Plate 625.
37. *Ibid.*, p. 371, Plan Figure 272, Plates 621, 630.
38. *Ibid.*, p. 377.
39. *Ibid.*, pp. 366–67, Plan Figure 271, Plates 618, 626. See also Peters, "Protestantsche kerkgebouwen," pp. 198–228.
40. Vermeulen, *op. cit.*, II, p. 360, Plates 619, 627.
41. Held, *Johann Valentin Andreae's Christianopolis*, p. 249.

CHAPTER THREE: *Reformation to Revolution:*
English Worship 1536–1643

1. Addleshaw and Etchells, *The architectural setting of Anglican worship*, p. 245.
2. *Ibid.*, p. 24.
3. Cardwell, *Documentary annals of the Reformed Church of England*, II, pp. 89–90.
4. Addleshaw and Etchells, *op. cit.*, pp. 30–36; and George Henry Cook, *The English mediaeval parish church*, pp. 266–68.
5. Gee and Hardy, *Documents illustrative of English church history*, Document lxxviii, pp. 439–41.
6. Frere, ed., *Visitation articles and injunctions of the period of the Reformation*, III, p. 62.
7. Addleshaw and Etchells, *op. cit.*, p. 146.
8. *V. C. H. Lancaster*, IV, pp. 257–58.
9. *Ibid.*
10. Calamy, *An account of the ministers . . . ejected . . . after the Restoration in 1660*, p. 401.
11. *Cal. S. P. Dom.*, 1672–73, pp. 504–5.
12. Addleshaw and Etchells, *op. cit.*, p. 52.
13. *Ibid.*, pp. 111, 113.
14. Whiffen, *Stuart and Georgian churches*, p. 10, Plates 4, 5.
15. Gee and Hardy, *op. cit.*, pp. 492–98.
16. Scheffer, *History of the Free Churchmen called the Brownists, Pilgrim Fathers and Baptists in the Dutch Republic*, p. 55.
17. Walker, *The creeds and platforms of Congregationalism*, p. 71.
18. Dexter, *The Congregationalism of the last three hundred years*, p. 308.
19. Ainsworth and Broughton, *Certain questions handled between H. Broughton and H. Ainsworth*, p. 11.
20. Francis Johnson, *A Christian plea conteyning three treatises*, p. 318.

21. Dexter, *op. cit.*, p. 316.
22. Burrage, *The early English dissenters,* I, p. 157.
23. Dexter, *op. cit.*, pp. 331–32.
24. "The Brownists Synagogue," p. 303.
25. Taylor, *The discovery of a swarme of Separatists,* n.p.
26. Frere and Douglas, eds., *Puritan manifestoes,* pp. 13–14.
27. Gee and Hardy, *op. cit.*, pp. 492–94.
28. Cardwell, *op. cit.*, II, p. 109.
29. Addleshaw and Etchells, *op. cit.*, p. 115.

CHAPTER FOUR: *Meeting Houses of the Middle Period:*
1643–1660

1. Chapter I, notes 19, 28.
2. Sudbury, Mass., 1643 (30′ x 20′); Springfield, Mass., 1645 (40′ x 25′); Cambridge, Mass., 1650 (40′ x 40′); Southampton, L.I., 1651 (30′ x 24′); Dover, N.H., 1652 (40′ x 26′); Easthampton, L.I., 1652 (26′ x 20′); Middletown, Conn., 1653 (20′ x 20′); Sudbury, Mass., 1653 (40′ x 24′); Watertown, Mass., 1656 (40′ x 40′); Norwalk, Conn., 1657 (30′ x 18′); Portsmouth, N.H., 1657 (40′ x 40′); Malden, Mass., 1658 (33′ x 33′).
3. For example, the drawings in Woodbridge, *Diary,* 1728, of the third meeting house at Deerfield, Mass., 1694. See Figure 22, below.
4. Crossley, *Timber building in England,* Figure 6.
5. Weymouth, Mass.; Dorchester, Mass.; Guilford, Conn.; Springfield, Mass.; Ipswich, Mass.; Newbury, Mass.; Haverhill, Mass.; Wethersfield, Conn.; Cambridge, Mass.; Southampton, L.I.; Easthampton, L.I.; Middletown, Conn.; Medfield, Mass.; Beverly, Mass.; Watertown, Mass.; Malden, Mass.
6. Moxon, *Mechanick exercises,* p. 159.
7. Powell, "Seventeenth-century Sudbury, Massachusetts," p. 7.
8. Neve (attr.), *The city and countrey purchaser, and builder's dictionary,* p. 141.
9. *Ibid.,* p. 128.
10. Willsford, *op. cit.,* p. 13.
11. Neve, *op. cit.,* p. 225.
12. Moxon, *op. cit.,* p. 165.
13. Donnelly, "New England pyramids, 1651–1705."
14. Scales, *History of Dover,* I, p. 120.

15. *The Bi-centennial book of Malden,* p. 123:

"... The said Job Lane doth hereby ... agree to build ... a ... meeting House, of Thirty-three foot Square, sixteen foot stud between joints. ...

"1. That all the sells, girts, mayne posts, plates, Beames and all other principal Timbers shall be of good and sound white or black oake.

"2. That all the walls be made upp on the outside with good clapboards, well dressed lapped and nayled. And the Inside to be lather all over and well struck with clay, and uppon it with lime and hard up to the wall plate, and also the beame fellings as need shalbe.

"3. The roofe to be covered with boards and short shinglings with a territt on the topp about six foot squar, to hang the bell in with rayles about it: the floor to be made tite with planks.

"4. The bell to be fitted upp in all respects and Hanged therein fitt for use.

"5. Thre dores in such places as the sayd Selectment shall direct, viz: east, west, and south.

"6. Six windows below the girt on thre sids, namely: east, west and south; to contayne sixteen foot of glass in a window, with Leaves, and two windows on the south side above the girt on each side of the deske, to contayne six foot of glass A piece, and two windows under each plate on the east, west and north sides fitt to conteine eight foote of glass a peece.

"7. The pullpitt and cover to be of wainscott to conteyne ffive or six persons.

"8. The deacon's seat allso of wainscott with door, and a table joyned to it to fall downe, for the Lord's supper.

"9. The ffloer to be of strong Boards throughout and well nayled.

"10. The House to be fitted with seats throughout, made with good planks, with rayles on the topps, boards at the Backs, and timbers at the ends.

"11. The underpining to be of stone or bricks, and pointed with lyme on the outside.

"12. The Allyes to be one from the deacon's seat, through the middle of the house to the north end, and another cross the house ffrom east to west sides, and one before the deacon's seat; as is drawne on the back side of this paper."

16. Brown, *The description and use of an ordinary joint-rule,* pp. 10–11, Figure 1.
17. *C. J.,* II, p. 287.
18. Winthrop, *Journal,* I, pp. 31–32.
19. Baillie, *The letters and journals,* II, p. 148.
20. *Ibid.,* p. 195.
21. *Ibid.,* p. 216.
22. Nuttall and Chadwick, eds., *From uniformity to unity,* p. 91.
23. Leishman, ed., *The Westminster Directory,* p. 78.
24. Calamy, *op. cit.,* pp. 125, 372, 477.
25. *V. C. H. Lancaster,* III, p. 148.
26. For Elswick, see *ibid.,* VII, p. 284; and for Sankey, *ibid.,* III, p. 410.
27. Dale, "Bramhope Chapel," pp. 325–34.
28. Mr. C. M. Mitchell, Director of the City Museum in Leeds, has found no documentation on the Bramhope pulpit but is of the opinion that on stylistic grounds it could "not be earlier than 1750" (private communication, March 23, 1964). A close parallel in style is the pulpit at Cottesbrooke, Northants., which local tradition dates in the early eighteenth century.
29. Calamy, *op. cit.,* p. 487.
30. *Ibid.,* p. 150.
31. Lawson-Tancred, "The township of Ellenthorpe and the Brooke family," p. 73.
32. *R. C. H. M. Essex,* III, p. 127 and Figure f.p. 127.
33. *Ibid.,* II, p. 106 and Plate f.p. 186.
34. Calamy, *op cit.,* p. 341.
35. Cleal, *The story of Congregationalism in Surrey,* pp. 17–18.
36. Betjeman, "Nonconformist Architecture," p. 163; and Calamy, *op. cit.,* p. 57.
37. Winthrop, *Journal,* II, p. 250.
38. *M. H. S. Colls.,* Series 4, VIII, p. 3.
39. *Ibid.,* pp. 4–5.
40. *Cal. S. P. Dom.,* 1656–57, pp. 382–43.
41. *V. C. H. Surrey,* III, p. 521.
42. *Cal. S. P. Dom.,* 1658–59, p. 176.

CHAPTER FIVE: *Meeting Houses of the Late Period: 1661–1700*

1. For an especially interesting discussion of this period, see Wertenbaker, *The Puritan oligarchy,* pp. 159–338.

2. Coffin, *A sketch of the history of Newbury*, p. 64.

3. Hamilton A. Hill, *History of the Old South Church (Third Church) Boston*, I, p. 274.

4. The English timber belfries remaining today are enclosed wooden towers, such as those found at Brookland, Kent, and Pembridge and Yarpole, Heres. This type of belfry is discussed in Crossley, *op. cit.*, pp. 38–49. Another possibility is an open timber frame-work, free-standing, of which there are Swedish examples at Skag-ershult, Närke, and Hackas, Jämtland (Lindblom, *Sveriges kuns-thistoria*, I, Figs. 79, 170).

5. *New England Weekly Journal*, April 28, 1729.

6. *Boston Weekly News-Letter*, March 6, 1729.

7. Hamilton A. Hill, *op. cit.*, I, p. 274.

8. Stiles, *Extracts from the itineraries and other miscellanies*, p. 264.

9. *Plymouth Church records*, I, p. xlix.

10. Currier, *History of Newbury, Mass.*, p. 337.

11. Powell, *op. cit.*, p. 13.

12. Corse, "The Old Ship meeting house in Hingham, Mass.," p. 22.

13. Embury, *Early American churches*, pp. 36–39; Place, "From meeting house to church in New England," pp. 74–76; Werten-baker, *op. cit.*, p. 110; Morrison, *Early American architecture*, pp. 80–81; Sinnott, *op. cit.*, pp. 32–35; and others.

14. Corse, *op. cit.*, p. 30.

15. *Ibid.*, p. 22.

16. Hoare, *The builder's pocket-companion*, p. 36.

17. Hamilton, *Gentleman's progress*, p. 167.

18. Thompson, *History of Long Island*, II, p. 613.

19. Stiles, *op. cit.*, p. 97.

20. *Records of the church in Brattle Square, Boston*, pp. 4, 9.

21. *Cal. S. P. Dom.*, 1660–61, p. 470.

22. Gould, ed., *Documents relating to the settlement of the Church of England by the Act of Uniformity of 1662*, pp. 386–404.

23. *Ibid.*, p. 395.

24. Whiting, *Studies in English Puritanism from the Restoration to the Revolution*, p. 334.

25. *Cal. S. P. Dom.*, 1661–62, II, p. 602; Gould, *op. cit.*, p. 464.

26. Gould, *op. cit.*, pp. 477–88.

27. *Ibid.*, p. 489.

28. Whiting, *op. cit.*, p. 57.

29. Wilson, *The history and antiquities of dissenting churches and*

meeting houses, II, p. 172.——In this connection the presence of a movable partition at the Gaol in York Village, Me., 1736, and the possibility of some kind of partition at the Whitfield House, Guilford, Conn., 1639, suggest the occasional use of such a dividing structure in buildings other than meeting houses. Efforts to find partitions discussed in the English builders' guides have so far been unsuccessful.

30. White, *The churches and chapels of old London,* p. 64.
31. *The records of a church of Christ, meeting in Broadmead, Bristol,* p. 158.
32. White, *op. cit.,* p. 43.
33. Turner, *Original records of early Nonconformity under persecution and indulgence,* I, p. 424.
34. Pevsner, *Wiltshire,* p. 176.
35. *Cal. S. P. Dom.,* 1667–68, p. 418.
36. *Ibid.,* 1668–69, p. 221.
37. *Ibid.,* 1667–68, pp. 85, 88; and 1670, p. 321.
38. *Ibid.,* 1668–69, p. 243.
39. *Ibid.,* p. 278.
40. Quoted in Waddington, *Surrey Congregational history,* p. 63.
41. *Ibid.,* p. 64.
42. Turner, *op. cit.,* I, p. 86.
43. Calamy, *op. cit.,* p. 478.
44. Waddington, *Congregational history, 1567–1770,* pp. 536–37.
45. Cardwell, *op. cit.,* II, pp. 333–36.
46. Cobbett, *Parliamentary history of England,* IV, pp. 561–62.
47. Turner, *op. cit.,* I, pp. 579, 567.
48. *Cal. S. P. Dom.,* 1673–75, p. 397.
49. Halley, *Lancashire: Its Puritanism and Nonconformity,* II, p. 246.
50. See for example the Presbyterian meeting house in Globe Alley, possibly c. 1672 (Wilson, *op. cit.,* III, p. 149).
51. To be built by Henry Tabor, carpenter: ". . . One new frame Edifice or building like unto the building knowne by the name of Mr. Ryther's meetinghouse . . . the said Edifice or building to containe in length from North to South fforty and six foot of assize little more or less and in breadth from East to West fforty foot to assize little more or less to be covered with plaine tiles; from the upperside of the Raizeing to the underside of the plate to be eighteene foot Item the Raizeing to be tenn and seaven inches, the Beames nine and eight inches, the King posts nine and seaven inches the

Basis seaven and five inches. Item the principal rafters tenn and eight inches, the purlings nine and seaven inches, the smale rafters three and fower inches, the maine posts nine and seaven inches, the punchions six and five inches, the Quarters two and three inches, the outside to be weather boarded with good deales; and tarred, and to be lined round within from the raizeing to the plate with two good kirt slitt deales, the ground plate with good oake five and nine inches. Item the ground floor to be laid with good yellow deals and oaken Joyces with a good brick foundation and to goe upp one stepp into the building, the Beames to be kneed and dogged with Iron. Item the principal rafters to be banded to the Beames with Ironplate, the Kingposts to be likewise banded to the Beames with Iron, and with sufficient lights and casements according to a draught . . . and to make three Double Doores with Locks, Keys, bolts, and hinges. Item to lay the windowes and doores twice in oyle colouring. The Edifice is to be plaistered over head . . . ." (Quoted in "Chapel building under the Stuarts," pp. 69–70.)

52. Gould, *op. cit.*, pp. 507–16.
53. *Ibid.*, pp. 515–16.
54. Briggs, *Puritan architecture*, p. 22.
55. For example, Knutsford, Brook Street Chapel, 1689 (described in Richards, *Old Cheshire churches*, pp. 376–77 and Figures 358, 359); Macclesfield, King Edward Street Chapel, 1689 (*ibid.*, pp. 379–80 and Figure 361); and Wilmslow, Dean Row Chapel, about 1693 in (Burgess, *The story of Dean Row Chapel*, pp. 21–24).
56. Briggs, *op. cit.*, Plates IIa, IIb, Figures 5, 6; and Godfrey, "The Unitarian chapels of Ipswich and Bury St. Edmunds," Plates VII, VIII.
57. "The ancient meeting-house at Walpole, Suffolk," photos f.pp. 316, 318; "The ancient meeting-house at Wattisfield, Suffolk," photo f.p. 250; and Godfrey, *op. cit.*, Plates I, XI.
58. Godfrey, *op. cit.*, pp. 125–26.

CHAPTER SIX: *The New England Meeting House as Puritan Architecture*

1. Rose, *The colonial houses of worship in America*, p. 463.
2. *Ibid.*, p. 192.
3. Crossley, *op. cit.*, p. 31.

4. Garvan, *Architecture and town planning in colonial Connecticut*, pp. 44–49.

5. Stone, *History of Beverly*, drawing p. 247.

6. Banks, *History of York, Maine*, II, p. 102.

7. Vermeulen, *op. cit.*, II, Plate 382.

8. See Gunther, *The architecture of Sir Roger Pratt*, pp. 92–97 for Coleshill, pp. 117–31 for Horseheath, and pp. 98–116 for Kingston Lacy. For Wisbech Castle and Thorney Abbey, see Webb, "The architectural antecedents of Sir Christopher Wren."

9. Forman, *The architecture of the old South: the medieval style*, p. 112.

10. *Rededication of the Old State House, Boston*, pp. 129–30.

11. Powell, *op. cit.*, p. 13.

12. Stephens, *The south Saxon diocese, Selsey-Chichester*, pp. 287–90.

13. Francis Johnson, *op. cit.*, p. 319.

14. Quoted in Porter, *The New England meeting house*, p. 5.

15. Winthrop, *Journal*, I, p. 75.

16. Purchas, *Purchas his pilgrims*, XIX, p. 55.

17. Scottow (attr.), "A narrative of the planting of the Massachusetts colony," pp. 307–8.

18. Jameson, ed., *Narratives of New Netherland*, p. 203.

19. Lechford, *op. cit.*, p. 78.

20. Edward Johnson, *op. cit.*, pp. 41, 67, 44.

21. Maverick, "A briefe description of New England and the severall townes therein," pp. 238, 245, 236.

22. Summerson, *Architecture in Britain 1530 to 1830*, p. 160 and Plate 98B.

23. *R. C. H. M. Buckinghamshire*, p. 341.

24. *Early Northampton*, pp. 27–28.

25. Pevsner, *Suffolk*, p. 224.

26. Pevsner, *Essex*, p. 177.

27. Powell, *Puritan village*, provides an interesting discussion of colonial village life.

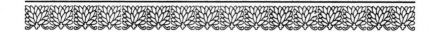

Bibliography

THE FOLLOWING are included in this bibliography:
1. Transcriptions of Town Records and histories of individual New England towns. (Manuscript records are listed for the individual towns in Appendix A.)
2. Seventeenth- and eighteenth-century New England writings.
3. Books and articles on New England history and architectural history.
4. Sixteenth- to eighteenth-century English and European writings.
5. Books and Articles on English and European history.
6. Books and articles on English and European architectural history.
7. Manuscript diary.

1. *New England Town Histories and Records*

Allen, Francis O., *The history of Enfield, Connecticut*. Lancaster, Pa., 1900.

Allen, Wilkes, *The history of Chelmsford*. Haverhill, 1820.

Anderson, Joseph, *The town and city of Waterbury, Connecticut*. New Haven: Price and Lee Company, 1896.

Ayer, Mary Farwell, "The South Meeting-House, Boston. (1669–1729)," New England Historical and Genealogical Register, LIX (1905), pp. 265–67.

Bailey, Sarah Loring, *Historical sketches of Andover*. Boston: Houghton, Mifflin and Company, 1880.

Banks, Charles Edward, *History of York, Maine*. 2 vols. Boston, 1931–35.

Barry, William, *A history of Framingham*. Boston: James Munroe and Company, 1847.

Bartlett, Josiah, *An historical sketch of Charlestown*. Boston, 1814.

Bell, Charles H., *History of the town of Exeter, New Hampshire*. Exeter, 1888.

The Bi-centennial book of Malden. Boston, 1850.

Bourne, Edward E., *The history of Wells and Kennebunk*. Portland: B. Thurston & Company, 1875.

Burt, Henry M., *The first century of the history of Springfield*. 2 vols. Springfield, 1898–99.

Caulkins, Frances Manwaring, *History of New London, Connecticut*. New London, 1852.

——, *History of Norwich, Connecticut*. Hartford, 1866.

Chapin, Alonzo B., *Glastonbury for two hundred years*. Hartford, 1853.

Chase, George Wingate, *The history of Haverhill*. Haverhill, 1861.

Coffin, Joshua, *A sketch of the history of Newbury*. Boston: Samuel G. Drake, 1845.

Crowell, Robert, *History of the town of Essex*. Essex, 1868.

Currier, John J., *History of Newbury, Mass*. Boston: Damrell & Upham, 1902.

Davis, Charles H. S., *History of Wallingford, Conn*. Meriden, 1870.

Dorchester town records. Fourth report of the Record Commissioners of the city of Boston. Boston, 1883.

Dow, Joseph, *History of the town of Hampton, New Hampshire*. Salem, Mass.: Printed by the Salem Press Publishing and Printing Co., 1893.

Early Northampton. Northampton, Mass., 1914.

The early records of Groton, Massachusetts. 1662–1707. Groton, 1880.

The early records of Lancaster, Massachusetts. 1643–1725. Lancaster, 1884.

The early records of the town of Dedham, Massachusetts. 3 vols. Dedham, 1892–99.

The first book of records of the town of Southampton. Sag-Harbor, N.Y., 1874.

Fox, Charles J., *History of the old township of Dunstable*. Nashua: Charles T. Hill, 1846.

Frothingham, Richard, *History of Charlestown, Massachusetts*. Charlestown, 1845.

Hanson, J. W., *History of the town of Danvers*. Danvers, 1848.

Hartford town votes. Collections of the Connecticut Historical Society, VI. Hartford, 1897.

Hill, Hamilton A., *History of the Old South Church (Third Church) Boston. 1669–1884.* Boston: Houghton, Mifflin and Company, 1890.

Huntington town records. Huntington, L.I., 1887–89.

Lockwood, John H., *Westfield and its historic influences.* Westfield, Mass., 1922.

Manuel of the First Congregational Church, Bristol, R.I., 1687–1872. Providence, 1873.

"Marblehead town records," *Historical Collections of the Essex Institute,* LXIX, 3–4. Salem, Mass., 1933.

Merrill, Joseph, *History of Amesbury.* Haverhill, 1880.

Metcalf, John G., *Annals of the town of Mendon.* Providence, R.I., 1880.

Milton town records. 1662–1729. Milton, Mass., 1930.

New Haven town records. 2 vols. New Haven: New Haven Colony Historical Society, 1917–19.

Orcutt, William Dana, *Good old Dorchester.* Cambridge: John Wilson & Son, University Press, 1893.

Plymouth Church records. 1620–1859. New York: The New England Society in the City of New York, 1920.

Portsmouth records. 1645–1656. Portsmouth, 1886.

Records of the church in Brattle Square, Boston. Boston: The Benevolent Fraternity of Churches, 1902.

Records of the colony and plantation of New Haven, from 1638 to 1649. Hartford: Case, Tiffany and Company, 1857.

Records of the colony of Rhode Island and Providence plantations, in New England. Providence, 1856.

Records of the colony or jurisdiction of New Haven, from May, 1653, to the Union. Hartford: Case, Lockwood and Company, 1858.

Records of the town of Braintree. 1640–1793. Randolph, Mass., 1886.

Records of the town of Brookhaven, up to 1800. Patchogue, 1880.

The records of the town of Cambridge (formerly Newtowne) Massachusetts. 1630–1703. Cambridge, 1901.

Records of the town of East-Hampton, Long Island. 5 vols. Sag Harbor, 1887–1905.

Records of the town of Plymouth. 1636 to 1705. Plymouth, 1889.

Records of the towns of North and South Hempstead, Long Island, N.Y. 8 vols. Jamaica, N.Y., 1896–1904.

Rededication of the Old State House, Boston, July 11, 1882. Boston, 1885.

Report of a committee . . . of Lexington. Concord, Mass.: Herman Atwill, 1922.

A report of the Record Commissioners of the City of Boston, containing the Boston records from 1660 to 1701. Boston, 1881.

Richards, Lysander Salmon, *History of Marshfield.* Plymouth, 1901.

Scales, John, *History of Dover, New Hampshire.* Manchester, N.H., 1923.

The second book of records of the town of Southampton. Sag-Harbor, 1877.

Second report of the Record Commissioners of the City of Boston, containing the Boston records, 1634–1660. Boston, 1881.

Sewall, Samuel, *The history of Woburn.* Boston: Wiggin and Lunt, 1868.

Shattuck, Lemuel, *A history of the town of Concord.* Boston, 1835.

Sheldon, George, *A History of Deerfield, Massachusetts.* 2 vols. Deerfield, Mass., 1895–96.

Stackpole, Everett S., *Old Kittery and her families.* Lewiston, Maine: Lewiston Journal Company, 1903.

Stiles, Henry R., *The history of ancient Windsor, Connecticut.* New York, 1859.

Stone, Edwin M., *History of Beverly.* Boston: James Munroe and Company, 1843.

Temple, Josiah H., *History of North Brookfield, Massachusetts.* North Brookfield, 1887.

Tilden, William S., *History of the town of Medfield, Massachusetts.* Boston, 1887.

Tilton, George H., *A history of Rehoboth, Massachusetts.* Boston, 1918.

Town records of Derby, Connecticut. 1655–1710. Derby: Sarah Riggs Humphreys Chapter, D.A.R., 1901.

Town records of Manchester, Massachusetts. Salem, Mass., 1889.

Town records of Salem, Mass. 3 vols. Salem: Essex Institute Press, 1868–1934.

Town records of Topsfield, Massachusetts. 2 vols. Topsfield, Mass., 1917–20.

Two hundredth anniversary of the Clinton Congregational Church. Clinton, 1867.

Watertown records. 8 vols. Watertown, Mass., 1894–1939.

Wenham town records. 1642–1706. Wenham, Mass.: Wenham Historical Society, 1930.

Whitaker, Epher, *Whitaker's Southold.* Princeton: Princeton University Press, 1931.

2. *New England Writings, Seventeenth and Eighteenth Centuries*

Cotton, John, *The way of the churches of Christ in New-England.* London, 1645.

Higginson, Francis, "New Englands plantation" (London, 1630), *Collections of the Massachusetts Historical Society,* I, 1806, pp. 117–24.

Hubbard, William, *A general history of New England, from the discovery to MDCLXXX.* Cambridge: Massachusetts Historical Society, 1815.

Johnson, Edward, *A history of New-England.* London, 1654.

Lechford, Thomas, "Plain dealing: or newes from New-England" (London, 1642), *Collections of the Massachusetts Historical Society,* Series III, Vol. 3 (1833), pp. 55–128.

Mather, Cotton, *Magnalia Christi Americana.* Hartford: Silus Andrus, 1820.

Maverick, Samuel, "A briefe description of New England and the severall townes therein," *Proceedings of the Massachusetts Historical Society,* Series II, Vol. 1 (1884–85), pp. 231–49.

Scottow, Joshua (attr.), "A narrative of the planting of the Massachusetts colony," *Collections of the Massachusetts Historical Society,* Series IV, Vol. 4 (1858), pp. 279–332.

Stiles, Ezra, *Extracts from the Itineraries and other miscellanies of Ezra Stiles.* Edited by Franklin Bowditch Dexter. New Haven, Conn., 1916.

Wadsworth, Benjamin, *Five sermons.* Boston, 1721.

Winthrop, John, *Winthrop's Journal* "History of New England" 1630–1649. New York: Charles Scribner's Sons, 1908.

———, *The Winthrop Papers.* 5 vols. Boston, Massachusetts Historical Society, 1929–47.

Young, Alexander, *Chronicles of the first planters of the colony of Massachusetts Bay.* Boston, 1846.

3. *New England History and Architectural History*

Calder, Isabel M., *the New Haven colony*. New Haven: Yale University Press, 1934.

Coolidge, John, "Hingham builds a meetinghouse," *The New England Quarterly*, XXXIX, 4 (December 1961), pp. 435–61.

Corse, Murray P., "The Old Ship meeting house in Hingham, Mass.," *Old Time New England*, XXI, 1 (July 1930), pp. 19–30.

Donnelly, Marian C., "New England pyramids, 1651–1705," *Journal of the Society of Architectural Historians*, XIX, 2 (May 1960), pp. 76–77.

Embury, Aymar, II, *Early American churches*. Garden City, N.Y.: Doubleday, Page & Company, 1914.

Forman, Henry Chandlee, *The architecture of the old South: the medieval style, 1585–1850*. Cambridge: Harvard University Press, 1948.

Garvan, Anthony N. B., *Architecture and town planning in colonial Connecticut*. New Haven: Yale University Press, 1951.

———, "The Protestant plain style before 1630," *Journal of the Society of Architectural Historians*, IX, 3 (October 1950), pp. 5–13.

Kelly, John Frederick, *Early Connecticut meetinghouses*. New York: Columbia University Press, 1948.

Morrison, Hugh, *Early American architecture*. New York: Oxford University Press, 1952.

Overby, Osmund R., "Architecture and the Protestant community," *The new community in Christ* (Minneapolis: Augsburg Publishing House, 1963), pp. 187–207.

Phippen, George D., "The 'Old planters' of Salem. . . . ," *Essex Institute Historical Collections*, I (1859), pp. 97–110.

Place, Charles A., "From meeting house to church in New England," *Old Time New England*, XIII, 2 (October 1922), pp. 69–77.

Porter, Noah, *The New England meeting house*. New Haven: Yale University Press, 1933.

Powell, Sumner C., *Puritan village*. Middletown, Conn.; Wesleyan University Press, 1963.

———, "Seventeenth-century Sudbury, Massachusetts," *Journal of the Society of Architectural Historians*, XI, 1 (March 1952), pp. 3–15.

Rose, Harold Wickliffe, *The colonial houses of worship in America*. New York: Hastings House, 1963.

Simpson, Alan, *Puritanism in Old and New England*. Chicago: University of Chicago Press, 1955.

Sinnott, Edmund W., *Meetinghouse & church in early New England*. New York: McGraw-Hill Book Company, Inc., 1963.

Thompson, Benjamin F., *History of Long Island*. Port Washington, N.Y.: Ira J. Friedman, Inc., 1962.

Thornton, John Wingate, *The landing at Cape Ann*. Boston, 1854.

Wertenbaker, Thomas Jefferson, *The Puritan oligarchy*. New York: Charles Scribner's Sons, 1947.

4. *English and European Writings, Sixteenth to Eighteenth Centuries*

Ainsworth, Henry, and Hugh Broughton, *Certain questions handled between H. Broughton and H. Ainsworth*. Amsterdam?, 1605.

Alberti, Leon Battista, *I dieci libri de l'architetture*. Venice, 1546.

Baillie, Robert, *The letters and journals of Robert Baillie, A.M.* Edinburgh, 1841–42.

Brown, John, *The description and use of an ordinary joint-rule*. London, 1686.

"The Brownists Synagogue" (London, 1641), in *Transactions of the Congregational Historical Society*, IV, 5 (May 1910), pp. 299–304.

Cardwell, Edward, *Documentary annals of the Reformed Church of England*. . . . 2nd edition. Oxford, 1854.

"Chapel building under the Stuarts," *Transactions of the Congregational Historical Society*, III, 1 (January 1908), pp. 60–71.

Eburne, Richard, *A plain pathway to plantations*. Edited by Louis B. Wright. Ithaca: Cornell University Press, 1962.

Frere, Walter Howard, ed., *Visitation articles and injunctions of the period of the Reformation*. London: Longmans, Green & Co., 1910.

—— and Charles Edward Douglas, eds., *Puritan manifestoes*. London: S.P.C.K., 1907.

Gee, Henry, and William John Hardy, *Documents illustrative of English church history*. London: Macmillan and Co., Ltd., 1896.

Gould, George, ed., *Documents relating to the settlement of the Church of England by the Act of Uniformity of 1662*. London: W. Kent and Co., 1862.

Hamilton, Alexander, *Gentleman's progress*. Chapel Hill: University of North Carolina, 1948.

Hoare, Michael, *The builder's pocket-companion*. London, 1728.

Jameston, J. Franklin, ed., *Narratives of New Netherland 1609–1664*. New York: Charles Scribner's Sons, 1909.

Johnson, Francis, *A Christian plea conteyning three treatises*. Amsterdam?, 1617.

Kerr, Hugh Thomson, *A compend of Luther's theology*. Philadelphia: The Westminster Press, 1943.

Kidd, Beresford J., *Documents illustrative of the Continental Reformation*. Oxford: The Clarendon Press, 1911.

Leybourn, William, *A platform for purchasers*. London, 1668.

Luther, Martin, *Luther's works*. Trans. by John W. Doberstein. Vol. LI. Philadelphia: Muhlenberg Press, 1959.

Moxon, Joseph, *Mechanick exercises*. 3rd edition. London, 1703.

Neve, T. (attr.), *The city and countrey purchaser, and builder's dictionary*. London, 1703.

Perret, Jacques, *Des fortifications et artifices*. Paris, 1594. Reprinted in German translation as *Architectura et perspectiva* (Frankfurt, 1602).

Purchas, Samuel, *Purchas his pilgrims*. Glasgow: J. Maclehose and Sons, 1905–7.

The records of a church of Christ, meeting in Broadmead, Bristol, 1640–1687. London, 1847.

Seventh Report of the Royal Commission on Historical Manuscripts. London, 1879.

Taylor, John, *The discovery of a swarme of Separatists*. London, 1641.

Turner, G. Lyon, *Original records of early Nonconformity under persecution and indulgence*. London: T. F. Unwin, 1911.

Vitruvius Pollio, *De architectura libri decem*. Edited by Daniele Barbaro. Venice, 1587.

Walker, Williston, *The creeds and platforms of Congregationalism*. 2nd edition. Boston: The Pilgrim Press, 1960.

Willsford, Thomas, *Architectonice*. London, 1659.

5. *English and European History*

The acts and ordinances of the Eastland Company. London: Camden Society, 1906.

Baird, Henry Martyn, *History of the rise of the Huguenots of France*. New York, 1895.

Burrage, Champlin, *The early English dissenters in the light of recent research (1551–1641)*. Cambridge: The University Press, 1912.

Calamy, Edmund, *An account of the ministers . . . ejected . . . after the Restoration in 1660*. Edited by Arthur Gwynne Matthews. Oxford: Clarendon Press, 1934.

Cleal, Edward E., *The story of Congregationalism in Surrey*. London: J. Clarke and Co., 1908.

Cobbett, William, *Parliamentary history of England, from 1066–1803*. London, 1806–20.

Cremeans, Charles Davis, *The reception of Calvinist thought in England*. Urbana: University of Illinois Press, 1949.

Dale, Bryan, "Bramhope Chapel," *The Bradford Antiquary*, n.s., Vol. I (1900), pp. 325–34.

Davies, Godfrey, *The early Stuarts, 1603–1660*. Oxford: The Clarendon Press, 1959.

Davies, Horton, *The worship of the English Puritans*. London: Dacre Press, 1948.

Dexter, Henry Martyn, *The Congregationalism of the last three hundred years. . . .* New York: Harper and Brothers, 1880.

Félice, Paul de, *Les protestants d'autrefois*. Paris, 1896.

Haag, Eugène, and Emile Haag, eds., *La France protestante*. Paris, 1846–59.

Halley, Robert, *Lancashire: its Puritanism and Nonconformity*. Manchester, 1869.

Hill, George, *An historical account of the plantation in Ulster*. Belfast: M'Caw, Stevenson & Cerr, 1877.

Lawson-Tancred, Sir Thomas, Bt., "The township of Ellenthorpe and the Brooke family," *Yorkshire Archaeological Journal*, Vol. 34 (1939), pp. 73–79.

Leishman, Thomas, ed., *The Westminster Directory*. Edinburgh and London: W. Blackwood & Sons, 1901.

Maxwell, William D., *An outline of Christian worship*. London: Oxford University Press, 1936.

Nightingale, Benjamin, *Lancashire Nonconformity*. Manchester: J. Heywood, 1890.

Nuttall, Geoffrey F., and Owen Chadwick, eds., *From uniformity to unity 1662–1962*. London: S.P.C.K., 1962.

Pannier, Jacques, *L'Église réformée de Paris sous Henry IV*. Paris: Librarie Ancienne Honoré Champion, 1911.

Phillips, Sir Thomas, *Londonderry and the London Companies 1609–1629*. Belfast: H. M. Stationery Office, 1928.

Rose-Troup, Frances, *John White*. New York: G. P. Putnam's Sons, 1930.

——, *The Massachusetts Bay Company and its predecessors*. New York: The Grafton Press, 1930.

Rowse, Alfred Leslie, *The Elizabethans and America*. New York: Macmillan Co., 1959.

Scheffer, Jacob Gijsbert de Hoop, *History of the Free Churchmen called the Brownists, Pilgrim Fathers and Baptists in the Dutch Republic 1581–1701*. Ithaca: Andrus and Church, c. 1922.

Stearns, Raymond Phineas, *Congregationalism in the Dutch Netherlands*. Chicago: The American Society of Church History, 1940.

Stephens, William Richard Wood, *The south Saxon diocese, Selsey-Chichester*. London, 1881.

Steyert, André, *Nouvelle histoire de Lyon*. Lyon, 1895–99.

The three charters of the Virginia Company of London. Williamsburg: The Virginia 350th Anniversary Celebration Corporation, 1957.

Waddington, John, *Congregational history, 1567–1700*. London: Longmans, Green, and Co., 1874.

——, *Surrey Congregational history*. London: Jackson, Walford and Hodder, 1866.

Whiting, C. E., *Studies in English Puritanism from the Restoration to the Revolution, 1660–1688*. London: S.P.C.K., 1931.

Wilson, Walter, *The history and antiquities of dissenting churches and meeting houses*. . . . 4 vols. London, 1808–14.

6. *English and European Architectural History*

Addleshaw, George W. O., and Frederick Etchells, *The architectural setting of Anglican worship*. London: Faber & Faber, 1948.

"The ancient meeting-house at Walpole, Suffolk," *Transactions of the Congregational Historical Society*, III, 5 (May 1908), pp. 317–18.

"The ancient meeting-house at Wattisfield, Suffolk," *Transactions of the Congregational Historical Society*, III, 4 (February 1908), pp. 251–56.

Betjeman, John, "Nonconformist architecture," *Architectural Review*, Vol. 88 (December 1940), pp. 161–74.

Briggs, Martin Shaw, *Puritan architecture*. London: Lutterworth Press, 1946.

Burgess, Walter H., *The story of Dean Row Chapel*. Wilmslow, Cheshire, 1924.

Cook, George Henry, *The English mediaeval parish church*. 3rd edition. London: Phoenix House Ltd., 1961.

Cox, J. Charles, *Pulpits, lecterns & organs in English churches*. London: Oxford University Press, 1915.

Crossley, Fred H., *Timber building in England*. London: B. T. Batsford Ltd., 1951.

Drummond, Andrew Landale, *Church architecture of Protestantism*. Edinburgh: T. & T. Clark, 1934.

Godfrey, Walter H., "The Unitarian chapels of Ipswich and Bury St. Edmunds," *Archaeological Journal*, CVIII (1951), pp. 121–26.

Gunther, R. W. T., *The architecture of Sir Roger Pratt*. Oxford: Oxford University Press, 1928.

Hamberg, Per Gustaf, *Tempelbygge för Protestanter*. Stockholm: Svenska Kyrkans Diakonistyrelses Bokförlag, 1955.

Hautecoeur, Louis, *Histoire de l'architecture classique en France*. Paris: A. Picard, 1943.

Held, Felix Emil, *Johann Valentin Andreae's Christianopolis*. Urbana: University of Illinois Press, 1914.

Innocent, C. F., *The development of English building construction*. Cambridge: Cambridge University Press, 1916.

Lewy, Max, *Schloss Hartenfels bei Torgau*. Berlin: E. Wasmuth, 1908.

Lindblom, Andreas, *Sveriges konsthistoria*. Stockholm: Nordisk Rotogravyr, 1944.

Merz, H., "Joseph Furttenbach. Ein Beitrag zur Geschichte des protestantischen Kirchenbaues," *Christliches Kunstblatt*, XXVII (1885), pp. 115–22.

Pannier, Jacques, *Salomon de Brosse*. Paris: Libraire Centrale d'Art et d'Architecture, 1911.

Peters, C. H., "Protestantsche kerkgebouwen," *Oud-Holland*, XIX (1901), pp. 198–228.

Pevsner, Nikolaus, *Essex*. London: Penguin Books, 1954.

———, *Suffolk*. Harmondsworth: Penguin Books, 1961.

———, *Wiltshire*. Harmondsworth: Penguin Books, 1963.

Richards, Raymond, *Old Cheshire churches*. London: B. T. Batsford Ltd., 1947.

Summerson, Sir John, *Architecture in Britain 1530 to 1830*. Baltimore: Penguin Books, 1954.

Vermeulen, Frans André Josef, *Handboek tot de geschiednis der Nederlandsche bouwkunst.* 's-Gravenhage: M. Nijhoff, 1931.

Webb, Geoffrey, "The architectural antecedents of Sir Christopher Wren," *Journal of the Royal Institute of British Architects*, XL, 14 (May 27, 1933), pp. 573–87.

Whiffen, Marcus, *Stuart and Georgian churches.* London: B. T. Batsford, 1948.

White, J. G., *The churches and chapels of old London.* London, 1901.

7. *Manuscript Diary*

Woodbridge, Dudley, *Diary.* October 1–10, 1798. Owned by Massachusetts Historical Society.

Index